Contents

1

The Animals Flew in Two by Two

The big Boeing jet from Singapore via India was alongside its allotted unloading ramp at the rear of Terminal Three at London Airport. Disembarkation was going smoothly, and the passengers were disappearing into the building on their way to Passport Control.

At the same time, as the last of the baggage was being cleared, a convoy of vans, fork-lift trucks, and low-loaders was assembling by the doors of the hold. When this was in position, there began a second and much stranger disembarkation of passengers. They hadn't a single passport between them, nor a piece of baggage, and if the original passengers now in the terminal had known what company they'd had on board with them from the Malacca Straits to the English Channel at 28,000 feet they might not have downed their gins, watched films, or dozed quite so easily. The second wave of passengers was the unseen airborne Noah's Ark contingent, the animals flown in as cargo on every routine flight from the Far East.

First off was a baby elephant, blinking in the daylight and looking a bit disorientated in his crate after his

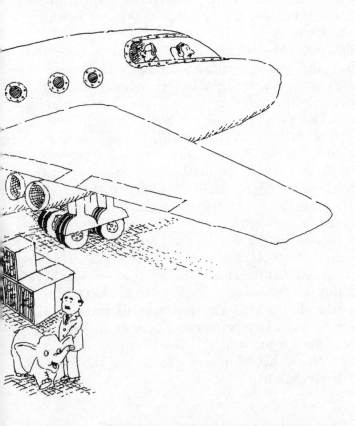

strange journey of thousands of miles to an even stranger land. Next was a consignment of 100 rhesus monkeys. They had joined at Delhi. After them, six Himalayan bears. Then a polystyrene box. This was packed with plastic bags filled with water which, in turn, contained Siamese fighting fish from Bangkok. Next, another large crate: 300 Java sparrows from Singapore. Finally, two smaller boxes containing dogs, the pets of two of the cabin passengers who had started their journey in Kuala Lumpur.

This was a quite ordinary live cargo from the Far East and India in the days when animal air traffic was at its peak, when London Airport was handling a million animals, reptiles, fishes, and birds a year. At this time, in the sixties, one in five of *all* passengers through Heathrow came into these categories. If I'd been a betting man, I could have made a fortune in those days wagering to the nearest hundred how many passengers certain airliners really carried, because the public hardly knew anything about the traffic.

At this point the human travellers simply collected their baggage and disappeared through Customs, or waited for a connecting flight, but the animals had a more complicated routine. If they were awaiting collection by dealers and other agencies in the U.K., or their onward flights were delayed by bad weather, engine trouble, wrong documentation, or strikes, they all came to the R.S.P.C.A. Hostel for Animals on the boundary of the airport near the old A4 Bath Road. Here they joined other creatures who had started in the U.K. and were waiting for flights out.

And this is where I come in, because for nearly twenty-five years I was the Hostel Manager. The R.S.P.C.A. started the Hostel despite the fact that, as an organization dedicated to animal welfare, it was frankly opposed to the traffic. The journeys of most of the creatures through Heathrow were seen as unnecessary. But they were legal, and the Hostel was started as a means of easing hardship and preventing suffering in unnatural conditions.

It was our job to see that animals got treatment equivalent to the airport treatment of human passengers – or better, since this wasn't always much of a standard to aim for. For many years after we opened, there were no international regulations governing the transport of animals by air. An enormous number came in for medical purposes, a lot for the pet trade, and others for zoos and collections. There was also a considerable traffic in English cattle and poultry, which was sent abroad for breeding purposes, and a lot of live food was imported, such as lobsters and turtles. Horses were transported to and from studs and racecourses in the United States, France and Ireland, even as far afield as Japan and Australia. In our time we looked after them all.

Because, in the earlier years particularly, there were no agreed standards of crating and packaging airborne livestock, the conditions some of the animals travelled in ranged from unsatisfactory to appalling. Partly because of our work, and publicity about the Hostel, and partly because of more enlightened public attitudes to animals, this has now just about been put right. Laws were passed and regulations agreed, and gradually these got tighter and tighter. At the same time there has been a reaction against the use of animals in medicine and research, a growing awareness of the need for wild life conservation, and at least a glimmer of recognition that keeping exotic creatures as pets is not in their best interests. As a result the traffic in mammals, birds, reptiles and fishes began to dwindle throughout the seventies. By 1981 the point had been reached where the Hostel was no longer needed, and it closed its doors.

During the three decades that we were needed, however, during which time millions of creatures passed through our doors, life was very worthwhile for me and my staff, almost entirely girls who were dedicated to their always hard and sometimes dangerous work. We had more than our share of drama, of pathos, of horror even. We also had our disasters, and a lot of laughter.

Above all, we never lacked variety. Every sort of creature imaginable appeared on our guest–list: aardvarks and African night owls, zorillas and zebra finches, killer whales, giant land snails, spitting cobras and a sick sea cow, to say nothing of linsangs (civet cats), pottos (relatives of the lemur), and on one occasion – when I didn't believe the cargo manifest because I thought the animal extinct – a relative of the zebra and ass from South Africa called a quagga.

Each morning when I arrived at the Hostel at eight o'clock I did the rounds and saw what had arrived overnight and been dealt with by the staff on night shift. I was doing this one summer morning and hoping, as always, that I would find something we'd never seen before. And I did. In the end stable of the building, stacked up, were thirty-eight wooden crates. In each of them was a Canada goose, very beautiful birds about three feet tall, which we'd never had at the Hostel before.

They were being exported to the Middle East, and were due out on an afternoon flight, so there was no need to take them out of their crates. They all seemed perfectly happy anyway, in very well-built travelling containers. But just after midday the airline rang up. 'Flight 402's delayed,' they said. The aircraft had developed some trouble they couldn't get to the root of. 'It could be a day or two before we're O.K. to go. Can you hang on to the birds till then?'

I asked the airline to give me the number of the export agents. I wanted it because as soon as I knew there was a delay, I decided that the Canada geese would have to be uncrated. I rang up and explained the position to the agents. I also asked, 'Would you mind if we turned the birds out into our paddock? There's about half an acre of grass and they'll enjoy being out in the sun.' The agents said that was fine.

So we uncrated the geese. Big as they looked, they were all very docile and tame. When the last of the thirty-eight had been released from its box, by which time the stable had just about a wall-to-wall carpet of geese, I opened up the door leading out into the paddock.

They made quite a sight as they paraded out like a Goosey Goosey Gander nursery picture, the sun catching the slate-grey and white of their heads. Forming a great gaggle, they proceeded with much dignity to the far side of the paddock, up to the fence running by the A4. They then turned, all looking across the paddock and beyond to where the expanse of London Airport stretched. On one of the runways a small private aircraft was taking off towards the hazy blue horizon. I felt pleased. The geese were obviously enjoying themselves and much preferred the paddock to being stuck in their crates. I watched for a few minutes, and was just about to go back into the Hostel when I suddenly noticed they had stopped preening themselves, ruffling their feathers, and generally looking round. Instead, they were beginning to form another line, and some of their wings were showing signs of movement. Had they seen the aircraft, and got ideas?

Maybe they had, because they all started moving in my direction, wings beating slowly, then faster and faster. I had a brief idea of what an eye-witness might have seen at the Charge of the Light Brigade. On they came. There was nothing I could do to stop them. I shouted. I waved my arms like a mad scarecrow. Still they came, and the leaders were now off the ground.

Ahead of them was the paddock fence, 10-foot-high chain-link with wire mesh. It was no obstacle. The leaders cleared it with a great clattering of wings, and the greatest of ease. I watched them, and almost unconsciously I counted them as they went... five... six... seven... eight. I watched as they got smaller in the blue distance, forming up into a shallow V. 'Eight...' I said aloud to myself again, and waited for the ninth, still shading my eyes and looking out over the fence. But there was no ninth. Instead of the regular beat of wings there was a confused sound behind me. I turned to see what was happening in the paddock, and I couldn't believe what I saw.

The majority of the Canada geese were still there, not airborne at all, but honking and milling about in goose-like confusion. Then I saw why their take-off had been abandoned. Mercifully, the wings of the geese still on the grass were pinioned. Those of the first eight – now

9

getting smaller and smaller over the horizon – had obviously not been.

Also getting smaller, I reckoned, were my prospects of carrying on in charge of the Hostel. How do you explain to the R.S.P.C.A., let alone the export agents, that you lost eight valuable Canada geese because you decided to let them out into your paddock? I was a very worried man as I turned back to the Hostel, the dole queue practically in sight.

But the story had an unexpectedly happy ending. After a long tussle on the phone with the agents I established that the birds should never have come to us without a warning note telling us their wings weren't pinioned. So it was the exporter's fault that they'd been able to fly. Then, a day or two later, we had reports that the geese had been seen on the reservoirs near Colnbrook, a few miles away. We recovered all but two.

These two were never caught. Instead they stayed around the reservoirs, and were frequently reported by commuters for a long time afterwards on a particular roundabout not far from the airport. So much so that they became a regular feature of daily life in the area, and if anyone remembers them from that time, they now know the reason why two Canada geese came by such a strange home!

A different kind of bird drama involved a box containing 300 budgerigars which was delivered to us off a Dutch aircraft. It was a fairly big box, several feet long and about two feet six inches wide and high; on the front was a mesh, with tins of drinking water. The budgies looked quite contented chattering and chirping away on their perches. There seemed nothing very unusual. But when one of the girls went to transfer the birds out of the box into our bird room, she noticed something odd, and decided to come and tell me.

'Mr Whittaker, there's something funny about that box the budgies came in. Can you come and look?'

I went down and had a look. It looked perfectly O.K. 'I can't see anything wrong.'

'Well, look at its size outside – and inside.'

I looked again. Then twigged. Its external width was two feet six inches, but inside it measured nearly a foot less!

'I'd better let the Customs know,' I said. The Customs were always telling us to be on the lookout for unusual ways of bringing contraband in, from Swiss watches to Indian hemp. I also knew that rare animals and birds were concealed sometimes. Smuggling them was big business at the time.

I went to the phone thinking, 'Old Crusty should have a field day here.' Old Crusty was the name we had in the hostel for one particular Customs man who almost always seemed to come down when we had trouble. If there wasn't trouble, Old Crusty could invent it, and usually did. He always reminded me of Spike Milligan's 'Mate' character in the Goon Show. In Customs terms his motto was: 'I don't care what the regulations sez, you can't park 'ere, mate.'

Sure enough Old Crusty came down with the scent of promotion in his nostrils – though he was long past it. He walked officiously round the box as if it might contain the Crown Jewels. He tapped it, bent down to put his ear to it, tapped again, and got the sound he'd hoped for. 'Hollow,' he said with a Sexton Blake-strikes-again note in his voice. Then he turned to me, summoning all the pomp, not to say pompousness, of his faded gold stripes: 'Would you mind opening the crate in my presence?'

Presence, I thought, that's a good word for Old Crusty. I got a hammer and chisel, went to work, and prised the back off the box. When finally it yielded we saw there was a false compartment, as expected. But this wasn't what really caught my attention. Inside were what appeared to be two largish sacks. Looking closer, I saw with a sick feeling that they weren't sacks at all. There, tied down in rough hessian, were a pair of king vultures, rare and handsome birds of prey with gaudy orange, purple and crimson heads; they come from Brazil, Mexico and the southern United States.

But, for one of them, all its finery had gone for

nothing. It was dead. The other had collapsed, and was barely alive. Two creatures condemned by human greed. Even Old Crusty was shocked.

The bird that was just alive I immediately transferred to our resuscitation cage. It was given intensive care, and within a few days, I'm glad to say, recovered. The Customs meanwhile issued a summons for smuggling, but because the birds came from abroad the R.S.P.C.A. found it harder to prove a cruelty charge. At least the Press gave the story a lot of publicity, and this, from our point of view, was the only good thing to come out of a shameful affair.

There then, are two stories to give some idea of the drama that was a constant factor in the life of the Hostel. What about the laughter? There was plenty of that when an ox-bird arrived one day. These little birds, about the size of a starling, live on the backs of the bigger African mammals such as buffaloes, elephants, rhinoceros, and, of course, oxen; they rid them of flies, fleas, ticks and other parasites, and in return for services rendered get free transport in the process.

Unfortunately, although there were plenty of occasions when we had elephants and rhinos in, this wasn't one of them, and we couldn't give the ox-bird his proper natural conditions. Instead, I had a frame made to roughly big African mammal proportions, and covered with sacking. This the ox-bird took to immediately, happily pretending he was riding along, pecking away, and living his normal life back in Africa. In reality he was in one of our bigger cages, but to give him some variety we used to release him into the bird room where he enjoyed his greater freedom – but would return immediately to his cage whenever one of us shook the sacking to attract his attention.

One morning, however, he found something even more attractive than his sacking frame. I happened to go into the bird room where he was flying about. No sooner had I got through the door than the ox-bird totally forgot what he had previously been doing. In a flash he zoomed down and made a perfect landing – in my beard!

Obviously this was a better substitute for a genuine ox's back than a bit of old hessian (although my beard may well have seemed like that as well). Once attached to my beard he set to work immediately pecking away in an effort to relieve me of any small livestock I might be carrying around.

Apart from giving me a bit of a shock at first, the ox-bird was no bother at all. From then on, every time I went into the bird room, the ritual was repeated, and I don't have to emphasize how the staff reacted (or how I did, for that matter) at the sight of the Hostel Manager stumping around looking like Long John Silver with a parrot that had slipped.

The lighter side of life sometimes involved excitement as well. One day we were warned to stand by for a famous film star. First a big Cadillac drew up with quarantine notices on the outside, and inside, lords of all they surveyed, two chi-hua-huas. The girls got the chi-hua-huas out and down to our quarantine kennels, and came back in double quick time to see a motorcade approaching with flashing lights, two carloads of Press photographers, and a posse of publicity people, agents and aides. From the leading car out stepped Jayne Mansfield in a pink knitted dress, looking every bit as I'd expected from the way she looked on the screen.

We were introduced. She fluttered her eyelashes at me and asked if she could see her dogs. With flash bulbs popping and the girls lining the route and taking it all in, the Hostel looked like a gala opening in Leicester Square.

The lighter side of life also, very occasionally, got mixed up with disaster. We had a call one night from a cargo superintendent down on the tarmac. His loaders were refusing to handle a cargo intended for us; could we go down to the aircraft? When we did, we found an Air Canada aircraft with its hold alive with timber ants. I immediately wished the ox-bird was still with us. He'd have had a field day. But he had departed long before.

The cargo of timber ants had been shipped out of Canada to Heathrow for onward passage to Sweden, and some genius had decided to pack the ants in hundreds – in wooden crates! All their boxes had been eaten through, and from the outside looked as if they were on their way to an exhibition of modern art. I couldn't help laughing. I then got down to the serious side. While the Disinfestation Squad dealt with the aircraft, I trundled the remaining crates back to the Hostel. Here we spent hours alternately trapping fresh break-outs of timber ants, and sealing their escape routes with industrial tape, all the time hoping we could contain them and prevent them taking over the entire Hostel before we could order steel containers the following morning. Luckily, we won the battle.

Long afterwards I was struck by an interesting thought about this unwelcome cargo. I realized that timber ants must have been the only creatures that Noah didn't allow two by two on board the Ark. If he had, who knows how the Bible story might have ended?

2

Boy on a Donkey

Animals have been my life. I first came into contact with them and learned to love them because I was lucky enough to be brought up by the seaside, in Blackpool, which, as Stanley Holloway's monologue says, 'is noted for fresh air and fun'. More important, it has the Blackpool Tower Zoo.

In the early twenties, when I was about four years old, my father, a P & O Line purser, left my mother. She went into domestic service in the household of a Fleetwood trawler owner called Noble, who had a big house at Cleveleys, between Fleetwood and Blackpool. I was sent to my paternal grandparents, who had an even bigger and grander house in Branksome, Bournemouth, with an entire river running through its grounds, and a host of domestic servants with whom I used to eat my meals and spend my life when not at school. School was a rather posh prep. place, and I remember my journeys home were quite happy events by the river. But then – for what reason I've no idea to this day, just as I've no recollection whatsoever of what my father's parents were like – I was sent back to live with my other grandparents in Blackpool, and that's where I spent the rest of my childhood. A lot is talked these days about 'broken homes' and how terrible the effect is. I can't say that I found it so very terrible – quite the reverse in fact.

One of the things I do remember very clearly to this day is the journey from Bournemouth to Blackpool. It was in my paternal grandfather's Bentley. And it was the very first of many journeys throughout my life in charge of a living creature. I travelled nursing on my knee my pet canary in its cage!

My new home was kindness itself. Grandpa was retired from being a night editor on the *Manchester Guardian*, because he'd been wounded in the back in the 1914–18 war. He had a daily routine which began, for reasons I never fathomed, with shaving himself in bed. He then dressed in smart tweeds and spats over polished brown shoes, and went for his constitutional, which took in the Kardomah Café for coffee and the Beach Hotel for a whisky and soda (always Haig – much later I would be despatched to buy Dimple Haig at 12s. 6d. a bottle for him). After that there would be bowls. The house was full of silver cups from the Bowling Club. Grandma was a bit like old Queen Mary to look at, although she didn't actually wear a toque. She could be as strict as her royal counterpart looked, but she was far from forbidding and if I did anything wrong, drawing 'I'll tell Grandpa' from her, nothing ever came of it. I was kept in order with a kind hand, and every morning, while Grandpa took salt with his unvarying porridge (which I couldn't stand), I always had bacon and eggs. It may not seem much of a luxury these days, but it was in the twenties.

Because of his back, Grandpa had an expensive bungalow built up near the South Shore, in Boscombe Road, and this is where we lived. Every Sunday my mother used to take the tram down from Cleveleys, an 8-mile ride, and come to see us. This was the day of the week I looked forward to most of all. She arrived, a petite figure with auburn hair, cheery despite all the disappointments and setbacks in her life, and there would be a hug and a kiss. After tea we both set off for the Waterloo Cinema, where we had a standing booking, to see the latest Laurel and Hardy (my favourite) or Clive Brook (her favourite, which I had to fidget through). I always saw her off on the last tram back to Cleveleys, at eleven – another bonus, because I would normally be in bed by that time.

There were soon other creatures apart from a pet

canary in my life. Hunting around the sand dunes, I became attached to the little sand lizards that sported round there; I even liked the shrimps and crustaceans I used to catch in the rock pools under the pier. But an even bigger attraction was the Golden Mile itself, the great stretch of entertainments that earned Blackpool its fame and fortune. What a place for a boy to grow up! In the school holidays I was there day after day among the Wakes Week holidaymakers from the Lancashire and Yorkshire mill towns, wearing hats bearing strange messages ('Kiss Me Quick' and 'Chase Me – I'm A Fire-Engine'), eating fish and chips, and mussels and cockles, pouring pennies into the sideshows, downing Bass and Guinness. They had the 'Good Time' that Blackpool offered, and put out of mind, for a week at least, the thought of mill looms, or worse, since the Depression was gathering pace, the threat that the mill gates might not even open up again when they got back home.

Life went by to the sound of Reginald Dixon at the organ of the Tower Ballroom playing 'I do like to be beside the seaside'. Who could resist it? I certainly couldn't, and I was drawn particularly to the sideshows that had animals in them. There was the Great Chief Bulawalbo who used to sit on a throne, chanting strange 'African' mumbo-jumbo, with tigers' teeth round his neck and plumed regalia, and, best of all, a 9-foot python. I happened to know that the Great Chief Bulawalbo, come the end of the season on the Golden Mile, went back to being a builder's labourer with a broad Lancashire accent, but it didn't spoil my fun. When his spieler called for volunteers to take the python round their neck, I was the one who volunteered, and sat up on the stage (for some reason I was never frightened of snakes, they just fascinated me), very proud of myself, with the snake as a live necklace, and part of the show as I drew Oohs and Aahs from the crowds.

The Great Chief, who affected no English but was a dab hand with a hod of English bricks, was billed as having been brought 'At GREAT EXPENSE from Africa to appear specially on Blackpool's Golden Mile'. It was not the only harmless con-trick practised by the showmen in the Barnum tradition of 'there's one born every minute'. Another was THE LARGEST RAT IN THE WORLD. This really was some animal. Its sub-billing was 'Caught in the Liverpool Docks', but it was pretty unlikely that the 'rat', which was almost certainly a coypu, had ever been nearer Merseyside than Blackpool itself. But no one in the crowd, me included, who came and paid to marvel at his size, really cared. There was also a ventriloquist with his ginger-headed dummy, and the famous Punch and Judy, not far from where the man, ablaze from head to foot, and hands tied behind his back, used to ride his motor cycle off the end of Central Pier into the sea.

But my first *real* contact with animals was not with pythons or giant rats. It was with the donkeys, who were such a huge attraction at Blackpool, as at all English seaside resorts. Blackpool has seven miles of sands, and it was here, over these long, truly golden stretches, that the donkeys jingled up and down among the beach shows. I became fond of one particular group of donkeys, mainly, I think, because they were the smartest and best turned-out donkeys of all the strings that used to 'work' the sands.

This group was run by a man called Bob, a roly-poly figure in black bowler hat, flannelette striped shirt-sleeves, an old black waistcoat that with wear had turned as shiny as armour, and a face as red as a brewer's almanac. I was about ten years old at the time, and when I was not at school I would more and more often seek out this immaculate little group of donkeys, with their polished harness and names in gold on scarlet leather headbands that I remember to this day...Daisy, Dolly, Jenny, Mary...

I soon became well known to Bob, his brother, and the two bare-footed lads who helped, because, when I'd spent my pocket money on a ride, I always used to hang about and get into conversation and wait with them till they packed up. In fact, during the school holidays, the thought of the donkeys took such possession of me that I used to leave Boscombe Road early with sandwiches in greaseproof paper packed up for me by Grandma, and go and spend the entire day down there, coming back tired, happy, and late.

'Now then, young Neville,' Bob would say, 'how's your pulse tick today?' The friendliness of Bob and the other lads was part of the attraction; they could so easily have been surly and told me when I asked a daft question to mind my own business and find some other donkeys to be nosey about. But they never did, nor ever made me feel a nuisance, which I probably was.

One day I saw that one of the lads was missing. During a lull in the donkey rides, Bob came up to me. 'How'd you like a job, young Neville?'

I felt suddenly excited. I thought: he wants me to stand in for the missing lad for the day. But it was better than that.

'How'd you like to work with us? There'll not be much money in it – a tanner a week at the outside, but if you want, you can start with us tomorrow.'

I can't remember what I said, except that, after getting over the surprise and the thrill, and making sure he wasn't having me on, I asked where I had to report for work, then before Bob could change his mind, pelted back home as fast as my legs would go.

'Grandma, Grandma,' I called, bursting through the door and going through the house like a small whirlwind.

'Whatever is it?' She came into the sitting room with a face looking for trouble. 'What have you been up to?'

'I've not been up to anything. I've got a job – with the donkeys.'

Her face relaxed. 'Go on.'

'I have really – honest. Can I borrow the alarm clock? I've got to be up at six.'

I felt very grown up, and it was the beginning of an era of magic.

In the morning (I'd set the alarm for five) I took the tram down to the London, Midland and Scottish Railway goods yard near the old South Station. I bought a

penny workman's return, realizing at the same time that
the investment, for a week, would eat up all my wages.
But I didn't care. When I arrived, Bob was already there
in the yard where the donkeys were stabled, and he
immediately put me to work: getting buckets of oats and
buckets of water, brushing the donkeys down, giving
spit and polish to the harness. No wonder Bob – and I,
too – were proud of *our* donkeys.

At 8.30 a.m. sharp we moved off. No cavalry troop
could have been better turned out as we trotted briskly
down to the sands, Bob or his brother in charge riding
side-saddle on the outside, nearest the tram lines, billy
cans on pommels, bundles of hay on the donkeys not
carrying anyone. I rode a donkey – or to be more
accurate, since she was a little larger than the rest, one
that was really a cross between a mule and a donkey,
appropriately called Jenny. The early holidaymakers
getting a breath of fresh air on the promenade all stopped
to watch us go trotting by. You really would have
thought we were the Horse Guards – and like a Horse
Guard I looked neither to right nor to left.

To make sure there was an even distribution of
business between the various strings of donkeys, Blackpool Corporation laid down that we should move in turn
up and down the beaches, so that each string had a chance
some time during a week to ply the most profitable
stretch which lay between North Pier and Central Pier,
opposite the Tower. When we were on this part of the
beach there was no pause in work: the sands were
thronged with the Wakes Week visitors from Bolton,
Bradford, Blackburn, Halifax and Oldham, expelled in
droves from the Bella Vista, Seaview, Sandiacre and a
thousand other boarding houses (they were allowed back
only for meals). There were queues waiting for rides at
twopence a time, and we took them all – except the
weightiest of adults (who fancied themselves either as an
oversize Steve Donoghue or Tom Mix, respectively the
current jockey and cowboy idol of those days).

With the adults – all out for a harmless good time,
shrieking with laughter even when they did (frequently)

the almost impossible and fell off – Bob had to be a bit tactful, but he did allow the donkeys to go a bit faster. With the children there was no problem; the donkeys knew to a yard, whether or not any of us went with them

with a 'Gee up, Mary' and 'Whoa there, Dolly', exactly how far to go up the beach before turning back, and when to stand sedately to unload their passengers and wait for the next ones.

When business was good the time flew by; Bob's leather pouch got fatter and fatter with copper coin and jingled in tune with the harness. There were, of course, the wet, windy days, when the donkeys stood with their backs to the weather, with us huddling beside them, and business was nil. The tides also affected how well we did. High water round about 6 a.m. and 6 p.m. was ideal. But high tide, say, at 11 a.m. meant a lot of waiting on the colonnade with no money coming in.

Sometimes, when we were up at the north end of the sands towards Cleveleys, or right down in the south on the Lytham side, and business was slack, we would have donkey races among ourselves. I rode Jenny and got her up to quite a speed – so much so that Bob was always saying when we dismounted, 'Young Neville, I think I'll have to enter you for the Belle Vue Donkey Derby.' I think he genuinely meant it, but, nothing was ever done about it, and sadly it remained a dream.

21

But what was certainly not a dream, and something to be looked forward to every day of that marvellous summer, was when the time came to pack up, with the sun getting low, and burning a red path over the Irish Sea, and the holidaymakers draining away up the beach back to the boarding houses, the pubs, and the Promenade. It was not just the simple thought of finishing work that was exciting, tired as I always was. It was the prospect of riding Jenny back to the stables – best of all when we finished up at the north end, and there was over five miles of exhilaration before home and the gates of the L.M.S. goods yard came in sight.

As soon as they did come into sight, the donkeys pressed forward to their feed after a hard day's work. A hundred yards or so from the entrance to the L.M.S. yard and the stables, I would feel Jenny's pace quicken, and, riding side-saddle with no reins, I knew I would really have to hang on. Quicker and quicker over the tarmac, and finally the stone setts of the yard, into a real gallop. How we all used to go, with a tremendous clatter of little hooves, and clanking of water buckets and billy cans, and hard luck for any holidaymaker who happened to be in the way: no time for snapshots then – only a moment to get out of the way of this excited horde with the scent of home in their nostrils. Then suddenly they would break back into a trot, and finally stand, panting and happy, awaiting the attention they knew they were going to get before we fed and watered them and said goodnight.

But all good things come to an end. School started once again, and in September I had to say farewell to the donkeys. My only consolation was that it was autumn – the Blackpool illuminations as sure a sign of this as falling leaves – and shortly the donkeys themselves would be making their final trip from their beach and would go away for a well-earned rest to their winter quarters.

School wore on, meanwhile, and I mean 'wore on'. I never liked it, not even the nature classes where there was some reference to animals. Only the thought of attractions beyond the schoolroom horizon kept me going. Each day I got a lift on the milkman's horse-drawn float as far as the school gates. There was next Easter and the donkeys to look forward to. Then there was Christmas, when I would go to Cleveleys and have a marvellous time with the Noble family and my mother. We were treated as part of the family, and when my mother had cooked the turkey we all opened our presents. There were two children about my age, and whatever they had in the way of presents from their parents, I got the same, whether it was a bagatelle table, a conjuring set, or a wrist-watch.

The other thing to look forward to was a bike. My mother had promised me a bike if I won a scholarship to the local secondary school. Much as I couldn't wait to leave school and be done with it, this was enough to make sure that I won that scholarship. I remember the evening the results came out in the local paper. Grandpa was scanning it in the sitting room when he called me: 'Neville. The results are in the paper.'

I went over and together we went down the column of small print. There, just as I was giving up hope, nearly last in the column, it said: 'N. Whittaker S.S.S.' S.S.S. were the initials of South Shore School, the one I was at.

But I wasn't thinking of the fact of winning the scholarship, nor of Grandpa shaking hands with his great warmth, and saying, 'Well done, Neville, I'll go and ring your mother.' I was thinking of that bike.

The following day my mother got time off and came down from Cleveleys, and we went to the cycle shop. My mother was thrilled about the scholarship, and nearly as keen as me when it came to looking over the rank of new bicycles which stood outside the shop front.

'Which is it to be, Neville?' Then, eyeing the price cards, 'Don't go off the deep end, will you love?' I knew what she meant. Three-speeds and dynamo lighting were out.

I chose a Hercules with drop handle-bars. Very racy. It cost £3 19s.6d. What I didn't know until years later was that she paid for it on H.P. at 1s.6d. a week. Her wages were only ten shillings a week. It was a very loving sacrifice.

The bike, when Easter came, gave me freedom from the tram down to the donkeys, and meant I could offer a penny or two of my wages towards my keep at Grandma's. If I'd known what I knew later I could also have helped to pay for the bike, but my mother never mentioned the subject. When I reported, an old hand, for the first day's work of the new season Bob gave me all the news. One of the things he told me was that one of the donkeys had a foal on the way.

If a donkey was nearing her time he naturally took her out of the line, and she was looked after in the stables until her foal arrived. Then, at a few weeks old, they both went to the beach; no sight caused greater excitement and interest than the mother donkey with her little foal trotting merrily and daintily beside her down the Lytham Road towards the Promenade. The box Brownies would be in force, and on the beach the little donkey would be in as much demand for photographs as a top model; children posed, their arms round its neck, and sometimes the very smallest even perched on the back of the new arrival.

It was about this time that my interest in animals took an entirely fresh departure. One Sunday, when my mother came along to Boscombe Road for her weekly visit, she looked in the paper to see what was on at the Waterloo Cinema and didn't fancy the film. So she decided to take me to the Tower Zoo instead. It proved to be a momentous decision.

The very first sight of that zoo, where I was to spend so much of my later life, is as vivid in my memory as it was then. I saw this cathedral-like, domed building, with huge cages either side, lined with clinical white tiles, with the lions and tigers, and the enormous cage full of monkeys. And from the moment that I walked in there and stood with my mother, a small figure in a school cap, catching the atmosphere and the noise and smell, I was drawn as if by a magnet, and something seemed to say: 'These are *your* animals, these are your friends.'

I was twelve at the time, and from that afternoon there was nothing I wanted more than to work at that zoo, among those animals. A year or so later, in 1931, when I was fourteen, I left school. Since my first visit, I had from time to time managed to scrape together the ninepence necessary to see the zoo again, and this had only strengthened my ambition. I'd done this by saving my wages, but my prospect of a bigger wage, as well as the work that my heart was set on, receded and dwindled to nothing with my first application after I left school. The zoo was fully staffed. Even worse, I was told I was too young anyway.

There was nothing for it but to look elsewhere for a job – not easy to come by because of the Depression – and bide my time. Eventually, I was taken on as office boy to a firm of heating engineers, a job in which there were two compensations. First, the wages were enough for me save up until I could buy a Rover Ticket, a sort of season ticket which cost £1 and admitted me whenever I wanted to the Tower Zoo, and also the variety bills at the Palace Theatre or Winter Gardens. Second, in the same street as the office I worked in was a firm of furniture removers, and their vans were pulled by magnificent Clydesdale horses. During my dinner break, I would go along there. I got to know the man in charge, and in time used to help look after them on a casual basis.

With my Rover Ticket I found I went far more frequently to the zoo than to the variety shows. I used to enjoy it particularly in the winter, when there were very few visitors in the evenings. Soon, because I went there so often, the keepers got to know me. The head keeper, who was called Bert, was a big man, built on the lines of a trawler skipper, and with an accent even further north than Lancashire. He used to discuss the animals with me, and the way they were looked after in the zoo. Even then I had formed views about the unnaturalness of zoos as a habitat for wild animals. I found that Bert didn't agree. He saw nothing wrong in lions padding about on polished mahogany floors, singly in their cages, and not in pairs as they would be naturally. As to feeding, he used to say, 'Well, you put the food down in front of them. That's all they want. They don't have to hunt for it.'

25

One day, Bert took me aside, and slightly conspiratorially, out of the side of his mouth, said, 'I've got a bit of news. There's a job going in the aquarium.'

This, at last, was my chance. Bert told me to get down to the staff entrance on the dot of nine the following morning.

I was there just after eight-thirty, so as to make sure. I'd told them in the office I would be out for about an hour. But it didn't take more than a minute for my hopes to be dashed. 'Sorry,' I was told, 'the job's filled, lad', almost before I got my head round the Curator's door. With a heavy heart I went back to the office to deal with the ledgers, and dream, when my attention wandered (which was fairly often), of animals dancing among the spindly, copperplate figures and accounts of profit and loss.

Not long afterwards I heard of another job, this time at the People's Dispensary for Sick Animals in Blackpool. I applied, and was interviewed by an important-looking man in a white coat. He squashed me even flatter than I had been at the Tower Zoo.

'But you've no qualifications,' he said.

'No,' I said, 'but I thought there would be training...'

He cut me short. 'Oh no, we don't do that. We need at least a degree in anatomy.' I was curtly shown the door.

I went out, thinking of what might have been. Grandpa had said, when he knew how really keen I was on animals, that they would try and get me through veterinary training. But the money never stretched to it, so there I was, being dismissed by a man in a white coat with no more thought than if he'd been swatting a fly.

That evening I decided enough was enough. I couldn't see any prospect of doing what I really wanted to do, whether with the P.D.S.A. or ideally, with the Tower Zoo. I'd reached the age of twenty. It was the autumn of 1938. Chamberlain had just come back from seeing Hitler with his promise of 'Peace in our time'. There weren't many, after the first feeling of relief that we weren't going to war with Germany immediately, who really believed him. It seemed no more than a postponement of the inevitable. I went to the Royal Navy Recruiting Office in Blackpool, and signed on.

Within a year I was serving in the first big warship to be sunk during the war, the aircraft-carrier H.M.S. *Courageous*. Luckily, I survived both this and another five years at sea – where the only animals I saw were ship's rats, ship's cats, and occasional monkeys and parrots picked up by the lads in foreign parts.

3

Into the Lion's Den

When I joined the Navy I went straight to the Recruiting Office and didn't tell either my grandparents or my mother until after I'd done the deed. I think they were all a bit shocked, because it was still, in theory at any rate, peacetime, and foreign commissions could last up to three years in those days. But my mother put a brave face on it and said, 'Well, if that's what you really want to do, love, I don't want to try and stop you.'

During the war we kept in touch by letter, although I must say I was never as dutiful as I should have been and I had more news from her than she got from me. Not that the demands of the war were too pressing for me to write when I was off duty. It was just inexcusable laziness on my part. But one day, early in 1945, when I was serving in the cruiser H.M.S. *Devonshire*, and working out of Devonport, I had a letter from her that had to have an immediate reply. She'd met a really nice man from Bolton, and she was going out with him. What about fixing a date for my next leave when we could all meet?

His name was Tom Gleason, and he managed a fish and chip restaurant in Lytham St Annes. He was a very quiet sort, with an angular face that could only come from Lancashire, and a broad accent to match. He used to listen very intently to whatever you had to say, and we immediately got on like a house on fire. We all went out to a pub for the evening, and when I got the chance I turned to my mother and said, 'I'm *really* pleased for you, mum.' She glowed with pleasure.

The next step was that they announced they were going to get married. Would I be their best man? I was delighted, and applied for compassionate leave to go up to Blackpool for the big day. The leave came through, and off I went. At the Register Office I think my mother was as proud of me as she was to be getting married again. I was in all my glory as a petty officer in best No. 1 blues with gold badges, and an assortment of the new campaign ribbons that had just come through. We had a party afterwards, and when I went on leave for the remainder of the war I used to go and stay with them.

Tom sold the Lytham business, mother left the Nobles, and they bought their own fish and chip business in Blackburn. The queues outside the shop every night were some evidence of what a master Tom was in the art of preparing and frying and serving. And he knew to an ounce just how much silver hake to slice in order to make a profit. When on leave I used to give him a hand, peeling the spuds, soaking them in bleached water in a kind of tumble drier affair so they kept their colour before going through the chip machine, and learning how to do the speciality of the house, which was called a Bulldog – a big potato carefully sliced, with fish in it, battered and fried – all for fourpence.

After the shop had closed we used to go down to the pub for a beer, always ending with a few scotches. Unfortunately, Tom suffered quite a bit with his stomach, and he'd turn to me and say, 'Neville, it's troubling me for nowt – I'll soon give it summat to trouble me for. Let's have a Scotch.'

Apart from staying with my mother and her new husband in Blackburn, when on leave I always kept up my connections with the Tower Zoo in Blackpool: I thought that when peace eventually did break out, there might still be a chance for me to do what I really wanted. The keepers that were left were over the age for military service and some of them quite getting on in years. I hoped that, come the time, if there was a job going there, they all knew me, and at least I would have a chance of being considered, qualifications or no.

Blackpool was a strange place during the war. Instead of the crowds of Wakes Week visitors, the front was full of R.A.F. cadets drilling up and down. But the day came when both they and I were demobbed. I went back to stay with my grandparents, and went straight to the Tower Zoo to see if there was a job. Nothing doing, so I went off to Blackburn for a time to help out with the shop and earn a bit of money over and above my demob. pay and gratuity.

Then, one day later in the year, when I was back in Blackpool, Bert, the head keeper, now the size of several trawler skippers but still as conspiratorial as ever, passed me the wire via the corner of his mouth that one of the other keepers was shortly going to retire, and there might be a job going. I remembered all those years ago, and an entire war in between, how he'd raised my hopes once before.

'Are you sure, Bert?'

'Well, I can't be absolutely *sure*. All I know is, if you play your cards right with the Curator, you should be all right. If I tell him, can you go and see him tomorrow morning?'

I spent a fairly sleepless night, and at nine o'clock sharp I was in the Curator's office. His name was Mr Pitt, and he was a very serious, elderly type, with stiff white collar and pin-stripe suit; he looked more like an accountant than somebody in charge of a zoo. He looked at me over his spectacles and told me about the job in a way that made me think I was back in the Navy listening to the skipper reading out the Articles of War at the start of a commission.

'It's very hard work,' he said. 'The hours are long, and the pay isn't exactly a king's ransom. It's no good if you don't have the nerve to go over the rails and into the cages with the animals. And you'll have to cope with the visitors. Some of them are moronic and frequently drunk, or both, and they'll try to intimidate you, if they get the chance, and try and make fun of you. Are you up to that?'

I said I thought I was.

'Why do you want the job?' The way he said it made it sound as if I wanted to put my head in a gas oven.

'Well,' I said, trying to sort out why I really did want the job very badly, 'I've always wanted to work with animals, particularly wild animals, and as far as I'm concerned there isn't another job in the world I'd rather do.'

He thought for a moment, sent me out, and called Bert into his office.

When I was summoned back after what seemed an age, all the years of disappointment and frustration rolled away. 'Right, Mr Whittaker,' said the Curator, 'We'll take you on and you can start at eight o'clock next Monday morning.'

I walked out on to the front, and the Golden Mile could really have been paved with gold!

Monday came at last. It was 27 August 1945, and it was the day I'd waited for ever since I left school. By ten minutes to eight I was going through the Long Bar of the Tower, which lies parallel to the zoo entrance, and along the centre aisle on my way to the Curator's office. Immediately, as a newcomer, I was given a greeting. But it wasn't the greeting I'd anticipated.

As I went, cage by cage, past the animals I knew so well by sight, each one in turn got up and eyed me intently. But that wasn't all. The lions started growling and padding restlessly up and down, tails swishing. The monkeys began an incredible chattering. The tigers snarled. I felt a tingle down my spine. The animals knew full well it wasn't yet time for the zoo to open. They also knew there was a stranger there in their midst; it made no difference that I'd been there scores of times before. I'd just been another visitor then. I knew at that moment I'd crossed a barrier, and no intention of friendship on my part could do anything about the hostility in the air. With arrogance and ignorance, I suppose, I'd always assumed that anybody could walk in, take a job, and look after these creatures. But now I knew it would take time for *them* to accept me.

I began to learn on this very first day the truth of what

the Curator had said in his interview. The job really was graft, and no mistake. I worked first with one of the keepers who was in charge of the 'small side': cheetahs, leopards, an extremely vicious black panther, and the little bears. He immediately despatched me with an empty half-gallon churn down to the local dairy to get the milk for the bears and the monkeys, who had bread and milk first thing in the morning. Next, armed with a tin of Brasso and polishing rags, I had to polish every last inch of the seemingly infinite brass rails, two of which, four inches in diameter, stretched the whole length of the zoo in front of the cages. It was a long business, which made me think for a wild moment I was back polishing brightwork in the Navy. This job had to be finished before 9.30 when the first customers bore like a tidal wave through the doors.

It was tedious but not difficult, except for one stretch. This was in front of the cage belonging to Reggie the lion. Reggie was named after the famous theatre organist, Reginald Dixon, whose name was synonymous with the Tower Ballroom. I don't think the human Reggie would have approved the honour if he'd known about his namesake's favourite party trick. This consisted of first attracting a great crowd round his cage. This he did simply by continuous roaring. He used to wait till the zoo was full of holidaymakers, and when he judged there were enough punters present he would roar so as to make the M.G.M. film lion sound like a laryngitis victim. His roaring was a daily feature of the zoo. The crowds jostled round until there was hardly room to move in front of Reggie's cage – another requisite condition for the party trick to come.

When he'd seen the audience had reached suitable numbers for the King of Beasts, and was packed solid with no hope of escape, Reggie would stop roaring, turn with great deliberation, and deliver his royal thoughts about Blackpool holidaymakers directly at them through the bars in a personalized stream of liquid. The panic was always incredible. Reggie had achieved his object. We, but possibly not the holidaymakers, thought it all good,

though not very clean, fun. But for whoever had to polish the rail in front of the cage there was a rich verdigris deposit to be got rid of every morning. Reggie watched me on the first day I polished his rail. It occurred to me that if he'd picked up a Lancashire accent while he'd been in Blackpool he would have said: 'Tha needn't think polishing yon rail will do thee any good. Ah'll see it's just as bad tomorrow.' And he always did.

So the day wore on, a pattern for all the days during my 'apprenticeship' at the zoo: a tea break in the head keeper's office, watched through a glass panel by two chimpanzees who gesticulated in apparent envy of my dripping sandwich; collecting half a crown's worth of damaged fruit in two buckets from the market, and dicing and chopping it; chopping meat up very fine for the insectivorous birds. Then, after lunch, helping the keepers to prepare for afternoon feeding time as they swept every speck of sawdust out of the cages, moving the animals along in succession from cage to cage, to make an empty one to work in. By the time I came to take my dust jacket off, I was whacked out. My view of wild animals had also been so changed that it would never again be the image I'd had since a boy.

Promotion came in stages. Looking back, it was really quite rapid, although it might not be thought promotion to have to do even more polishing. As a junior keeper, however, after only a week or so, I was put to work polishing the great brass padlocks which were three feet up on every cage door. The first time I did this, thinking I ought to take out shares in Brasso, I knew the animals would try and test me, just as they'd shown hostility on my first morning. I had to get over the brass safety rail, and go right up to their cages, something I'd never done before.

I saw and heard the signs as soon as I approached the rail and made to get over it. There were instant growls. Reggie lunged forward. There were snarls and hissings, and every animal was suddenly on its feet pacing about. And the more they snarled, the more I didn't want to get over that rail. Then Bert appeared. 'Go on, Neville,' he said, 'now's your time. Over you go.' So over I went, armed only with a Brasso tin and a bundle of cotton waste, and ran the snarling gauntlet right the way down to Peggy the tigress, normally the most placid of animals, who was showing that she could be ferocious with the best of them. Finally it was all over. The padlocks gleamed, and I went back for a tea break with a new understanding of what early Christians must have felt like in Rome.

The next step was being put in charge of the smallest animals for feeding time. This saw me up on the roof gardens with the rabbits and guinea pigs, cleaning out the budgerigars, and seeing to the other birds, the cranes, parrots, parakeets and cockatoos. All the time the ever-watchful eye of the Curator was upon me, to keep me from getting too proud of myself.

When he wasn't on the prowl, warning, 'Come along, Neville, that's not good enough, you know', he was seated in his favourite vantage point on the bench down the centre aisle, looking more than ever remote from the zoo, and more than ever like an accountant on a day out. He would spot a drunk trying to climb the safety barrier inflamed with a desire to stroke the black panther and would immediately shout, 'Neville! On the double! Get that drunk out of here!' He himself would never stir from his seat; he simply directed operations against drunks, who could be more aggressive and dangerous sometimes than any of the animals.

The visitors to Blackpool Zoo were pretty incredible. The scene as they came in at the height of the season when the doors opened in the morning – particularly on a wet day when, turned out of the boarding houses, they'd nowhere else to go except a soaking pleasure beach – was like a cast of thousands in a Cecil B. de Mille biblical epic, doing the bit where all the swine rush headlong over the cliff. Once inside they all checked in their stride and clapped handkerchieves to their noses, with a sort of mass 'Phee-ew' sound.

This daily ritual was something you just had to put up with. We all thought it totally unnecessary. There was obviously a smell of animals in the zoo. But there was nothing objectionable about it, and everything was spotlessly clean and well kept – we had callouses to prove it. Maybe we were just more used to the aroma, I don't know. What I do know is that this was only a beginning.

One of the holidaymakers' tricks was attempting to make Reggie roar. As already seen, he didn't need much encouragement, and in any case always got his revenge. They tried to make the monkeys jump up and down in their cages. They also offered lighted cigarettes to the monkeys who, trusting and friendly, rarely failed to take up the offer and got their paws burnt to the sound of much laughter. Another trick was to offer the monkeys apples on open pocket-knife blades. Whereupon more merriment as the monkeys cut themselves.

Despite big notices warning 'These Monkeys Like Spectacles' people allowed their specs to be grabbed off their noses through the bars of the cage, and the monkeys suffered the consequences when they broke the lenses and had to be taken to have their paws stitched. We often thought we knew best who should really be in the cages – and it wasn't the animals. Sometimes we could get our own back. Among countless questions we would be asked, 'What does this one eat?' We always replied, 'Money! Throw it in to him!' And we swept up the dividends later.

During the winter we worked shifts. Instead of starting at eight in the morning, I was on duty from two in the afternoon till ten-thirty in the evening. It was at this time, when there were very few visitors, particularly in the evenings, that I realized how monotonous and sad the life of the animals was. During the day there was a bit of daylight, but no fresh air; at night there were only bare electric bulbs for light. In the silence of the winter evenings I used to go round and see the animals, far from their natural habitat, with nothing to occupy them. None of them, including a bear who had been at Blackpool for fifteen years, had anything to look forward to but this barren existence. It made me sometimes feel more like a prison 'screw' than a zoo keeper.

The following spring there was further promotion. The Curator called me in and told me I was to take over the monkeys. As I walked away from his office and the idea sank in, I realized that this was a real step up. The primates had always been my favourites in the world of wild animals.

The keeper in charge was about to retire, a process which had been hastened by the monkeys themselves, nearly forty occupants of the large pagoda-shaped cage, and monkeys of all kinds, rhesus, African greens, mona monkeys and sooty mangabeys. For some reason the occupants of the pagoda had decided that the keeper was fair game, and had taken to mobbing him when he went into their cage, jumping on his head, pinching the pen out of his pocket and generally ganging up on him – all of which wasn't as playful as it may sound, because some of the monkeys could be quite dangerous, and were experts at biting ankles and calves. No wonder some keepers wore corrugated cardboard inside their trousers as a precaution.

This knowledge rather cooled my ardour about my latest step up the zoo ladder, although it didn't prevent me looking forward to the challenge. I knew that the monkeys somehow must have sensed that their previous keeper was losing his power of control over them, and that I had to make sure there was no nonsense from the very beginning. I also welcomed the advice which was forthcoming from other keepers, the most significant of which was contained in two words: 'Watch Billy!'

Billy was a very senior rhesus monkey; if the monkeys had been capable of doing graffiti, the cage would certainly have been chalked with 'Billy Rules O.K.'. He was a kind of Al Capone among monkeys, not much to look at, but absolute in his power over his own underworld. He had a red face, a red backside, and one single pickle tooth remaining in his cunning head. His

back legs had gone, so he couldn't climb the bars of his cage like the younger ones; but he more than made up in authority for the loss of youthful bounce. Whatever Billy did, the others would follow: 'Be aggressive,' Billy might dictate, and there would be much teeth baring. Or, 'Be nice to the gentleman', and all would be fine.

Sometimes the younger monkeys would get out of

hand, little realizing that Providence in the ungainly shape of Billy could be tempted only so far. Billy would sleep on the cage floor, and the little ones found it was a fine game to swing off their perches, bounce on Billy's stomach and on to the floor – and then up the bars and back for another round of the same again, and again, and again. Until Billy decided he'd had enough. He would then wearily rise, lumber decisively on all fours across to the bars of the cage, and shake and shake and shake them, until every small monkey was back on its perch or on the floor, and every eye was on Billy, and order was restored. Billy would then mooch back and resume his rest.

'Nobody moves,' was his Capone-like motto, 'until I say so.' Particularly when it came to eating. Not a monkey dared take a mouthful until Billy slowly raised his hand to his mouth and his eyes grudgingly signalled, 'O.K. you guys.' Then they all fell to, but, if there was a squabble over the food, Billy was across instantly to cuff some order back into the proceedings.

So I knew the first confrontation would make or break me in Billy's beady eyes, and in those of every other occupant of the pagoda cage. 'Don't take any chances,' were the last words to me as I prepared for the ordeal.

'I won't,' I said, but the confident tone mocked me as I heard the door of the cage drop shut behind me. Immediately, to show who was boss (me, rather than Billy, that is), I banged the handle of my broom sharply down on the cage floor. Billy, who had already started advancing towards me, halted in his tracks. He was baring his teeth, admittedly, but apart from this show of his own authority to the other monkeys he made no aggressive signs that would have instantly called the mob down on me.

I remained where I was. Billy remained where he was. He looked at me. I looked at him. Then Billy called it a day. He turned and started with much dignity towards the other side of the cage. This was a signal for attention from the other monkeys, released from the All-Powerful Influence.

'Hello Bimbo,' I said to one of the little monkeys I knew. Bimbo responded by poking me immediately in the eye. He meant no harm, he meant no harm, I thought, as my eye began to stream, blurring the vision of the crowd of other monkeys coming over to make their number with me, climb on my shoulders, and altogether show as much friendliness to me as they had shown aggression to my predecessor. It was a good start – but I was glad that I'd got Billy on my side!

My time with the monkeys lasted several months, and all went well. So much so that I knew that it wouldn't be long before I got further promotion, and I could be measured for my coveted dark blue and gold braided suit, and at last wear the cap that announced officially to the world that an ambition had been achieved. In one word of golden lettering it would say it: 'KEEPER.'

4

Danger: Animals at Work

During the autumn of 1946 the big moment arrived: promotion to full keeper. Greater responsibilities were balanced by the glory of being able to walk around with the keys to *all* the cages, including the 'big side', the lions and tigers. From now on I could go into any cage I wanted at will, and at any time: something I'd hankered after from the minute I joined the zoo. With it went the uniform, all bright blue and new gold braid. As I went into the zoo, I was conscious of cutting a fine figure.

If it impressed the paying customers it certainly didn't impress the animals. They were no fools, and they could spot a dude from the genuine article a mile off. Far from letting me cut a dash, their idea, I very soon learned, was to cut me down to size. It was just like my very first morning when they showed that the right to authority had to be earned with their respect. On this morning they set about showing that a uniform is only as good as the man inside it.

Lesson one came from Anita, the lioness. Swinging my new bunch of keys, I was going grandly past her cage where she looked to be fast asleep, a bit like a female version of the picture on the Lyle's Golden Syrup tin, only with zzzz's instead of bees buzzing round her head. Just outside the front of her cage I spotted some sawdust. Now sawdust was something that the Curator would not tolerate. When he wasn't seated in his usual position on

40

the bench bawling orders at us to get rid of drunks, he was prowling up and down peering in the cages for specks of sawdust. It obsessed him in the way that first lieutenants in my time in the Navy were obsessed with rust on the ship's side, and used to go berserk at the sight of the smallest spot of it.

On this occasion, however, the Curator was nowhere to be seen. I decided that this was the moment to try out my new authority. With Anita still looking out for the count, I was quickly over the safety barrier, picking up a broom, and sweeping in the gap between the bars and the floor of the cage. I'd reached one end, with Anita behind me, when I heard a sort of swish, and at the same time felt a terrible shock of pain in my wrist. Anita, far from being asleep, was wide awake. She had lashed out one of her great paws and ripped my wrist open. Blood spurted as I whipped round and faced her through the bars. Anita gazed back at me, and if there was any expression in her eyes it meant 'Serve you right'.

Holding the wound, and trying not to get too much blood on my new uniform, I leapt back over the brass safety rail and into the Curator's office where the first aid was kept. I didn't get any sympathy there. The Curator, sitting at his desk, merely expressed what Anita couldn't say. As I poured the Dettol and applied the lint and bandage, he said: 'I'm surprised at you, Neville. I thought by now you knew the number one rule: *never* take your eyes off the animal.' To this day I have the scars as a permanent reminder of Anita's lesson, to say nothing of the text from the Curator's safety first sermon.

After Anita, it was the turn of Rajah, the tiger. Rajah was a really magnificent beast, a Siberian tiger even more imposing than the more commonly seen animal from India. Rajah and his mate Peggy (officially called Miracle on her cage because she had miraculously survived a terrible illness) were given water three times a day. It was put in a metal dish between the foot of the bars and the cage floor; the dish had a special lip, or raised flange, on one side, to prevent it being dragged into the cage.

I slid the dish into the cage and filled it with water from

a watering can. Rajah padded forward and started lapping up the drink. So far, so good. But when he'd finished and I came to take the dish out again it wouldn't move. I saw that Rajah had stealthily managed to clamp just a single claw of his immense forepaw over the rim of the dish. I tugged. I yanked. I grabbed and pulled with both hands. Nothing happened. Rajah eyed me with the sort of look I imagined Nazi interrogators had when they knew you were going to submit and give them the plans. I desperately heaved again. I shouted at Rajah. I banged at the cage bars. A small crowd was beginning to gather, and, in my shining uniform, I was beginning to feel fairly ridiculous as, no matter what I did, Rajah kept his claw firmly in place.

I grimly pulled again with all my strength, thinking that whoever had designed the dish not to go into the cage had never foreseen it might one day be impossible to get out, when suddenly, causing me to fly backwards against the safety rail, it was free. As I crashed against the brass barrier the dish flew in the air, and my new cap saying 'KEEPER' jerked down over my eyes. The crowd loved it.

I didn't care. When I'd put my cap straight, I saw Rajah was retreating almost apologetically to the other side of the cage. I'd won. The crowd might laugh (and did) but they'd seen who was boss. With great dignity I turned to recover the dish. As I did so I came face to face with the keeper who had previously looked after Rajah. In that moment I knew I hadn't won at all. He had seen what was happening, come up behind me, stood four square to the cage, and, without a word, just *glared* at Rajah. Rajah, in turn, had known that this was a trick that would never work with an old hand. I felt like the apprentice who, on his first day, has been conned into going to the factory store to get a ball of chalk.

One of the most important lessons a zoo keeper has to learn is that however much you may love the animals, you can't be too careful. We had two newly imported and very valuable gibbons who lived in a cage next to the pagoda cage where most of the monkeys were. Gibbons come from the great tropical forests of Asia. They have abnormally long arms, which they use to swing swiftly from tree to tree. In their cage in the Tower Zoo bars had been specially fitted so they could indulge their natural climbing habits.

Normally gibbons are gentle, affectionate creatures with a natural liking for the company of human beings. They are friendly, and not given to 'monkey tricks'. But these two were different. They were getting on in years, and, whether captivity had soured them or not I don't know, but at best they could be niggly, and at worst like a pair of cantankerous old codgers.

I decided I needed a bodyguard when I went in to feed them. As they swung up and down the bars, did trapeze-artist imitations, and dropped from roof to floor almost quicker than the eye could follow, I knew they were capable of getting down, nipping you in the neck or swiping you over the head, and being out of reach in a twinkling. So I always took another keeper in the gibbons' cage with me. He would sit on the lowest parallel bar of the cage as I fed the two quicksilver fur shapes, with a broom ready, and watching for trouble. Because of this I managed to avoid a fractured skull or perforated neck to add to my other wound.

The two chimpanzees we had, called Adam and Eve, also presented problems. With the bear, the chimpanzee has been labelled the most potentially dangerous creature in any zoo. The bear is dangerous because his face is totally expressionless: there is no way of telling his intentions, which might be strictly honourable, or, on the other hand, all for a big hug of not the most loving kind. Chimpanzees are dangerous because of their uncontrollable tempers. They remain my favourites among all the primates, but by the time I was in charge of them I knew that there could never be any spirit of give and take between us. I admired them for all sorts of reasons, but I knew that the flashpoint of losing their cool was very low indeed, and that once the fuse had blown a lot of damage could be done in only a few seconds.

Adam and Eve lived in a special cage next to the head keeper's office, with a glass panel let in to the side of that office from their sleeping quarters and glass inside their bars. It was, in fact, Adam and Eve who watched me – and, more particularly, my dripping sandwich – on the very first day I joined the zoo. Normally the head keeper looked after them, but I was to be trained to do so as well, and therefore had to make their acquaintance other than through a glass panel.

Accordingly, one evening, it was decided that I should 'go solo' with the chimps. We waited until the holidaymakers had gone, knowing that the public, from those in the Colosseum of ancient Rome to the customers at Chipperfield's Big Top of the present day, like nothing better than anticipation of disaster, and preferably a death or so. I had no desire to be a sacrificial spectacle. I knew the 'form', having seen the head keeper go into Adam and Eve's cage many times. Their performance was unvaried. As soon as the head keeper went in, their normally sleek hairs would stand up like bristles; they would beat their arms about, jump up and down, and advance on him. He, meanwhile, would have locked the door behind him and, observing a golden rule, put the key in a safe inside pocket. As Adam and Eve advanced he would bang his broom handle sharply on the cage floor and rap out two words of command that would have done credit in a Guards' barracks. 'ADAM ... EVE' he would bark. Immediately the two chimpanzees would stop their show of aggression. I knew what I was in for and my stomach turned over as I approached the cage.

I was thinking of their sheer strength, for a start, let alone mere displays of aggression. From the roof of their cage hung a long manila rope with a big knot at the bottom. They would use this knot as a foothold, climb to within three feet of the roof, reach up an arm, insert a finger into a small hole in the roof, and, totally free of the rope, suspend themselves by that finger to demonstrate their strength! They would then let go, drop the twelve feet to the floor, and walk away as if they had done nothing unusual. As I approached the cage, I was all too aware that I had nothing beyond a broom should anything happen. In emergency, the head keeper used to keep in his pocket a very short length of rubber hose with which to deal a salutary whack about the body should a really extreme need arise – though the sight of him going for his pocket was usually enough for Adam and Eve to stop whatever they were doing.

All seemed well, however. Adam and Eve were both asleep on their floor, looking like rather overgrown Babes in the Wood, beguilingly innocent. I turned the key in the lock and quietly let myself in. The transformation scene was incredible: from Babes in the Wood to demons in less than a second. I was no sooner in the door than they were on their feet, hair standing up, arms waving, doing vertical take-offs, and, worst of all, limbering up to run the length of the cage towards me. In less time than it takes to write this, they were charging headlong. I was rooted to the cage floor, petrified! Don't move, I told myself. And then, in time – just – I remembered a word or two of advice the head keeper had given me. I stood facing them as they loomed larger and larger, and deliberately put my right hand in my dust coat pocket. Then, with equal deliberation, I drew my hand slowly out. The effect was miraculous, even without a length of hose. Adam and Eve abandoned their charge, stopped dead in their tracks, and just stood a foot or so away facing me, saying in unison, 'Uh-uh-uh-uh.' Which, roughly translated, means: 'All right, all right, you've made your point. It's O.K., we're all friends.'

I silently released a long breath of relief, walked across to the front of the cage, sat on the ledge which runs round the outer part, and waited for the next move in continuance of Solidarity, Friendship, Goodwill, etc., etc. I hoped it would come, and it did. First Eve, then Adam, hairs now restored to normal sleekness, ambled across. Eve was interested in my wrist-watch, fingering it thoughtfully, then picking at it. Adam liked my finger nails and gave them some attention. He looked at me intently all the time. For this I was grateful. If a chimpanzee takes your hand and faces you, O.K. If he starts bringing his arm to his mouth, on the other hand, head for the hills. But Adam and Eve, after demonstrating their ritual show of aggression against an intruder, a stranger in their home, were very content to demonstrate friendship. So we got along famously for this first meeting, and I was almost sorry when I saw the head keeper coming into the cage, saying 'Time for bed', and bringing Adam and Eve their goodnight mugs of milk and half a loaf each of Hovis.

Life seems very much worth living after an encounter of this kind. But the good feeling I had when I stepped out of Adam and Eve's cage that evening into the deserted zoo was as nothing compared with the relief I felt not long afterwards, following a visit to another cage, that of Tessa, the Malayan sun bear.

Sun bears are smooth-coated little bears, not more than four feet tall, amusing, even comical, by nature. From the Malay Peninsula, Borneo, Sumatra and Java, they are addicted to honey. This is their main delicacy when in the wild, and only when they cannot get at a bees' store do they go for other sugary substances as a substitute. It was Tessa's sweet tooth, allied to human idiocy, that was my undoing.

I had gone into her cage to mend a sheet-metal panel she had over her door – or, to be more accurate, to secure it back in position after her strong, sharp claws had prised it away from the bars. She was her normal self when I went in, an affectionate creature. She came up and licked my face. When I started work, she went snuffling round, no doubt dreaming the sun bear's permanent dream, particularly in captivity, of a land flowing not with milk and honey, but just with honey, from horizon to horizon. While my back was turned – it was in the morning, and the zoo was already filling with visitors – Tessa's dream came partly true. Some well-meaning visitor who obviously knew the particular likings of sun bears, and chose to ignore the notice on Tessa's cage which stated 'Do NOT Feed the Bear', threw a jar of honey through the bars. Unfortunately, it landed an inch or two away from my tool bag. Tessa spotted the jar immediately and made straight for it, grabbing it and beginning to try and scoop out the food she hadn't seen for years. Honey even in those days was very expensive, and the zoo budget didn't stretch to it.

At that very same moment I turned round, not really looking what I was doing, to feel for a hammer in my bag. It was too much for Tessa. She thought my hand was competing for her pot of honey. To be living a lovely dream one moment, and the next to have it threatened, turned her from an affectionate little creature into a raging monster. She went berserk. I saw her come for me, and in a split second realized what was happening. I dropped the hammer, nails and pliers and made straight for a dead apple tree which providence had placed in anticipation, perhaps, at the centre of her cage. Tessa raged across after me, screaming like a thousand banshees, and stood at the foot of the tree as I, not a moment too soon, shinned to safety. And there she remained, the pot of honey forgotten, simply concentrating rage and screams on a hapless figure in a blue uniform clinging to the tree. Her screams were so loud that they were apparently heard outside the zoo in Bank Hey Street. They certainly brought visitors flocking. Soon there was an arc of gaping holidaymakers more than a hundred strong round the cage, and a fine cartoon spectacle they enjoyed.

But the screams attracted not only the visitors, and those rubber-necking for the disaster that would have made their day. Out of the corner of my eye, pushing and elbowing his way through the press of people beyond the bars, I caught sight of another keeper. He pushed and shoved his way through the crowd, and I saw he was armed with a shovel. As soon as he got through, he started banging his shovel against the bars. The screams stopped. Tessa turned, and lumbered off in the direction of this distraction. While her back was towards me I seized my opportunity. I was down the apple tree quicker than a lightning strike, across to the door, and out. There was a great murmur from the crowd: whether of relief on my behalf, or disappointment at being baulked of further more horrific drama, I don't know. I did hear one distinct comment, though: 'Doesn't he look *white*!' said a voice.

It was the only laugh I got out of the incident, and that only in retrospect. Yet there *was* other laughter in the zoo. Much of it was caused by Adam and Eve. After my first visit to their cage, I used to make it a practice to go in alone in the mornings, before the zoo doors were open, and we quite soon got used to each other. This was all in preparation for me taking my turn to be in charge of the Chimpanzees' Tea Party.

The Tea Party was a daily event, advertised on the doors for 4 p.m.; it was the most popular feature in the zoo, attracting great crowds. The same criticism can be applied to chimpanzees' tea parties, I suppose, as to other instances of animals being trained to do what they would not naturally do, but the saving factor as far as chimpanzees are concerned is that they really do seem to take part naturally – when sunny tempered that is – and enjoy the whole mad business.

The trick with the chimpanzees was to have the nerve to show that although you knew you were in *their* cage, it was *you* that was boss. My morning visits to Adam and Eve got me used to them, and watchful for their every move despite their friendliness after the ritual aggression. I knew, for example, that one of them would be sure at some point to go and try the cage door to see if, by

49

chance, I had forgotten to lock it and put the key in a safe pocket. And when they thundered down from the ceiling I was careful not to be caught between them and the cage bars: a deft blow in this trapped position might have done no good at all for my looks.

The training for the Tea Party included similar precautions, despite the seeming light-heartedness of the proceedings which the crowd (little did they know) took for granted. My morning visits provided time for the rehearsal for the afternoon routine. At eight o'clock I moved in the table and stools, and Adam and Eve had their proper breakfast (in contrast to the food they had in the afternoon for the benefit of the visitors), which consisted of bread and milk. I 'waited' on them, correcting them if they didn't put their cups back on the saucers as they had been trained to do, or tried any other tricks. It was like teaching children table manners.

By the time I first took over the Tea Party, the chimpanzees and I were great friends, and I was so used to the rehearsal routine that I took it in my stride. Soon after three o'clock, when the other animals were being fed, into Adam and Eve's cage would go the table, and stools, the cups, saucers and plates, and the tablecloth. Finally, as four o'clock approached and the crowd had gathered, I would take the food in: oranges, grapes, bananas, bread and, most important, what looked like delicious chips of the kind that would have done credit even to my Mum and Tom's shop in Blackburn. The sight of those 'chips' struck a chord with the holidaymakers, and Adam and Eve always ate them so fast the game was never given away. They never gave the 'chips' a chance to turn brown and show up for what they really were: cunningly sliced apple.

On our first 'run' with the Tea Party routine all went well, and, to be fair to Adam and Eve, it normally did subsequently. The chimps used to delight the audience with impeccable manners that would not have been out of place in a vicarage. Sometimes, however, things didn't quite go to plan. Adam, in particular, liked occasionally to remove a 'chip' from the dish, and take a sip of milk with all the daintiness he was capable of. Then, instead of replacing his cup in his saucer as he'd been taught, he would put the 'chip' on the table and attempt to balance his empty cup on it. When it refused to balance, he would turn the cup into a useful hammer and smash the 'chip' to smithereens. Roars of laughter from the audience.

I had to check this without the crowd realizing, and, more important, without upsetting the chimpanzees so that they started playing up even more. I would move my right hand forward towards the cup. 'Look Adam,' I would say, in the sort of deliberate language used in small children's comics, 'put...it..on..the...sau-cer...' Adam usually did as he was told, but on one occasion he had different ideas. Without any warning, he bit me through the palm of my outstretched hand. I was so surprised that beyond a stifled 'Ouch' I showed no reaction whatsoever. I think, for the benefit of the audience, I even laughed. Adam by now had gone back to vicarage manners. So the crowd round the cage never suspected what had happened, although they might have wondered at the end of the performance why the keeper took out all the crockery and stools, and dragged the table, with one hand only.

This was only a minor lapse, and never repeated. But it was a small monkey bite to Adam and Eve's notion of a grand finale to their show. This happened only once to me, though other keepers were not so lucky. Just as the chimps' tempers could snap like a frayed hank of cotton, so their concentration could also go, and it was sometimes difficult to keep them behaving perfectly towards the end of the Tea Party. I saw the signs one day. Adam and Eve were becoming more and more like children getting restive and bored with sitting up at table, and were playing with their food in the way known to all parents. Any minute, unless I brought proceedings to a close, I knew they were going to show off. But I wasn't quick enough.

Eve yawned and refused to drink the last of her milk. Adam was waving a banana skin in one hand while delving about in the last of the 'chips' with the other. I was about to correct him, when suddenly they had had enough. As one they jumped from their stools. Eve up-ended the table, and a shower of cups, saucers, plates and assorted uneaten fruit hit the cage floor. Adam deftly grabbed the tablecloth. I was taken unawares, and as I rose, meeting a tide of wreckage halfway, Adam and Eve took off round the cage in a wild game of Catch the Tablecloth. Round and round they went, uttering chimpanzee sounds meaning 'Hooray, this is better than a silly party'. The audience, thinking it was all part of the show, gave roars of encouragement and laughed themselves sick.

There was, of course, no option but to let them think it really was all part of the act. So, while the mad chimpanzee merry-go-round continued at ever more hectic pace, I managed to clear up the debris, and pass the stools and table through the door to another keeper who was waiting. When I'd finally cleared it all, I let myself out; neither the audience nor Adam nor Eve either noticed or cared. The tablecloth had at last been caught. As I turned the key in their lock from the outside, I could see that for the curtain call it was about to be torn to shreds in an enthralling tug-of-war.

Chasing one another came quite naturally to Adam and Eve, and I myself was not averse to joining in their fun and games. Quite apart from my morning visits, I used sometimes to go into their cage in the evenings when the zoo had quietened down a little and not many visitors were about, and my object was purely to be sociable. Sometimes there would be a chasing game, and I would be the object of pursuit; at others I would chase the chimpanzees – with what effect on the visitors the other side of the bars I neither knew nor cared. No doubt it made a talking point or two in Bolton and Bradford in the long winter evenings.

When all our energy had run out I used to sit on the ledge that went round the cage. They would then simply come up and be friendly, and do their usual thing of examining me, and my pockets, minutely. This was happening one evening when the door of the cage opened and in came the Curator. Adam and Eve knew him very well, so he, too, was made welcome as he came over to the ledge for a chat.

Adam did a ritual inspection of the Curator's jacket, including the pockets. Eve seemed more interested in his hair. But eventually their interest waned and they ambled off, leaving us talking. Outside the cage, beyond the glass front and the bars, I could see the evening visitors strolling about. Looking into the chimpanzees' cage was a little boy with his mother. They were still there a moment or two later when I glanced out, but to my utter astonishment they had been joined by someone else. At first I thought it was a trick of reflection in the glass but a rapid check inside told me that only Eve was left in the cage. It really *was* Adam out there, placidly standing beside the little boy and holding his hand. Equally placidly, the little boy seemed to think there was nothing unusual about it all.

That wasn't exactly my reaction, nor that of the Curator when I silently gestured outside to tell him to look. Firemen answering a 999 call couldn't have got out of the cage quicker than we did. At the same time I realized what had happened, and it was some compensation for being lectured on safety when Anita tore my wrist. Even the Curator, I was pleased to note, sometimes broke the golden rules. He'd broken the one that concerned coming into the chimpanzees' cage. It was just a pity that I hadn't the nerve to remind him. He'd quite correctly locked the door from the inside. But he hadn't taken the key out of the lock and put it in his pocket. That key was truly a key to Adam's personal ambition. He'd seen time and time again what happened when we came through the door, and time after time had gone in vain for the key. This time he'd been lucky, and he made the most of it.

Freedom, once gained, is worth fighting for. Neither a curator – admittedly not the most menacing of figures in pin-stripe suit and starched collar – nor a keeper could be allowed to stand in the way. Adam spotted us as soon as we hurtled from the cage towards him. Instantly he dropped the little boy's hand, and in a blur of furry movement was up on the brass safety rail, and disappearing along it at a rate of knots towards the far end of the zoo, arms outstretched like a professional Big Top tightrope artiste. But this performance was nothing to the effect it had on the rest of the inmates of the zoo. As Adam loped and teetered past cage after cage, every animal in turn did the equivalent of a double-take, and, not believing what it saw, reacted accordingly. The little monkeys went wild, chattering and screaming, and swinging wildly round and round their pagoda. The gibbons did somersaults. Rajah snarled and charged the bars of his cage. Reggie thought it was time to repeat his daily party trick. Everything at this normally quiet time came to life and set up the most unearthly racket.

We were no more than supporting cast in the entire bizarre spectacle: the Curator of the zoo, no less, plus one uniformed keeper, running at a safe distance behind a runaway chimpanzee! I say 'safe' because whatever we did we knew that a chimp on the loose was one thing, but an angry chimp on the rampage would earn us headlines we could do without. We followed Adam to the other end. He alighted, nimble as a ballet dancer, from the rail. This was our chance. We closed in. But no. Conquering one brass rail and creating total uproar was not enough. There was another rail on the opposite side. That way lay further freedom, and, with just two or three bounds, Adam was up and away and careering back in the opposite direction, accompanied by another hideous crescendo of snarls, shrieks, and chatterings as he went. The Curator and I said not a word, but simply followed again. At the end of the rail was the Curator's office. Adam came to this natural terminus, stood swaying on the rail for a moment, did one or two acrobatic tricks, then caught sight of us approaching.

With not a gesture of defiance, nor any outward sign, he simply jumped down, ambled good-naturedly up the aisle towards us, took the Curator by one hand and me by the other, and together we all walked back to his cage. The door was opened. Eve was there to greet him with a sort of 'My hero' look in her eye. And Adam just went in, content with a memory that would last him all his days.

Life in the Tower Zoo, fairly naturally, was not all excitement of this kind, but even the routine provided variations and interest. Time went by, and I added all the time to my experience of the animals – from having to sleep in the cage with young tiger cubs who were ill and had to be injected regularly throughout the night with antibiotics, to dealing with enquiries from the R.S.P.C.A. about cruelty to our resident Russian bear. This originated in the idiocy of visitors who threw toffees into his cage which he rolled on. They stuck all over his fur, and eventually resembled sores, which well-meaning people decided to report.

Time ticked on. The seasons rolled by seemingly in a flash. I realized one day that I had been at the zoo for nearly five years; I was so much a part of it that when I went in the White Swan close by for a pint my entrance was always greeted by the landlord's dog howling for all he was worth, because by then I was so impregnated with the zoo smells. Sometimes I used to think that I ought to move on, even though I was perfectly happy and content. But where would I move to? What more did I really want to do? On a spring day in 1950 came the answer to both questions.

5

On the Boards

One Sunday afternoon during the 'little winter' season between Easter and Whitsun I was on duty in the zoo. There were hardly any visitors, and most of these were local people. Leaning on the brass safety rail I was answering their questions: How long do the animals live? Do they feel lonely? Is it difficult to be a keeper? I felt like the original *Wonder Book of Why and What*. Then I noticed someone approaching who looked out of the ordinary, not at all the usual kind of visitor: a short, thickset man wearing a bright overshirt and check trousers, with a natty line in black and white buckskin footwear of the kind that used to be known as 'co-respondent's shoes'. He walked up briskly and immediately started in on the questions. These, like his appearance, weren't at all usual: How long have you been with the zoo? Did you work with animals beforehand? What kind of animals are you most experienced with? I gave him the answers, or as much as I wanted to tell him, and wondered who he was.

At last he introduced himself. His name was Pepino. He was an animal trainer, and he had an act touring the variety circuits. Then he came to the point: 'How would you feel about joining the act, and working with me?'

It sounded, on the face of it, an intriguing idea. Ever since my days of going to the Palace Theatre and Winter Gardens with a Rover Ticket I'd been fascinated by variety. Even so I didn't go wild or fall on my knees at the offer. I said, 'Thanks. Can I think it over?'

It wasn't the first approach I'd ever had from an animal

trainer. There had been the great lion tamer, Konyeti, who had wanted me to go on tour with him and his Abyssinian lions to the States – but on eleven dollars a month. I'd also had an offer from a chimpanzee act going to do a summer season at Great Yarmouth. In this case, not only was the money no good, but I didn't fancy Great Yarmouth either. But there was something about Pepino, perhaps his directness, perhaps the air of being unmistakably boss of his own animal act, I don't know, and when he suggested we should have a further talk I agreed.

So when I went off duty that evening I made my way along to the Queen's Hydro on the South Promenade and met Pepino again. This time his wife Olga was with him. She had been a trapeze artiste, also helping her husband in his act. They lived in Blackpool, and that week 'Pepino And His Miniature Circus', as they were billed, were appearing on home ground at Feldman's Theatre (later re-named The Queen's). Pepino told me more about his act, prompted where necessary by Olga, and gave me a signed card that would let me into Feldman's any time during the coming week to go and see for myself. Then he said, 'Do you want to come and see the animals now? They're not far away.'

'Why not?' I said, because I'd already begun to take to Pepino. He not only knew what he was talking about, but I could tell he really cared for animals.

So we had another Scotch for the road and set off to see the animals. They were in a paddock very near some familiar territory from my boyhood days with the donkeys, not far from the old L.M.S. goods yard. The first thing that caught my eye as Olga, Pepi – as she called him – and I approached was a big blue van of the size used for furniture removals. On it, picked out in white with vivid, extravagant scarlet scrolls and curlicues, was 'Pepino's Miniature Circus'. But the sight was nothing to the sound that greeted us.

From inside the van came an assortment of excited barks, whines and yelps, with a sort of descant of neighing, that grew to a symphonic frenzy as Pepi started undoing the rear door. He opened the door, then prepared to let down the tailboard, but, before this could happen, out leapt an enormous dog roughly the size of the Hound of the Baskervilles.

It was Peggy, the Great Dane. She made a wild fuss of Pepi and Olga, then sniffed me all over with a mad wagging of her tail. It was immediately plain that anything further from a Hound of the Baskervilles in temperament would be hard to find. Like so many big dogs, Peggy was affection and softness through and through. Beyond her flailing tail, inside the van, I then saw the rest of this mini-menagerie. There was a black and white pony who returned to munching at her hay-net after looking at us in greeting. This was Flicky. A little above her and along the sides of the van were boxes with grille fronts. This was where most of the noise was coming from: a Heinz range of little mongrel dogs. Pepi opened up their boxes, and out they jumped in a sort of canine cascade, scampering and barking round and round. Finally there were two monkeys, a rhesus similar to Billy but younger (and, I hoped, not as cantankerous) and a vervet called Diane. Diane came to the front of her cage, and Pepi warned: 'Don't touch her Neville, whatever you do. She's a bit unpredictable till she gets to know you.'

So I stood there watching this strange circus exercise and take titbits from Olga, and as I did so I tried to weigh things up. One thing was clear: it looked a happy sort of outfit.

'Well, what do you think, Neville?' asked Pepi.

'They look fine,' I said, not wishing to commit myself yet.

After we'd been there a few minutes Mike arrived. He looked after the animals and was going off to another job, hence Pepi's slight urgency to get a replacement settled. Mike was told who I was and explained in a broad Tipperary accent what he did. Not only that, he took his time over it. So much so that I could see straightaway that if he did his work as speedily as he got to the point Pepi would not be too upset over losing him. Cutting out the friendly, rambling by-ways of the conversation, it boiled down to: 'Exercising the dogs, seeing to the feeding, grooming Flicky, and doing your stuff with them on stage.' He gave me a big grin: 'That's about it in a nutshell.'

I grinned back and thought, 'Some nutshell.'

I decided to walk over to Pepi and broach the one subject that had not so far been mentioned: wages. Pepi led me away from the van and made his offer. He proposed to pay me a fiver a week, plus insurance and unemployment stamps. In addition, if ever the act was booked on the basis of a percentage of theatre profits, I would get a bonus according to how much business we did. Now £5 a week was good money in those days. At the zoo I was getting thirty bob (£1.50) a week. There was a bit of difference. I shook hands with Pepi and said I would let him know as soon as I could.

When I got home I told my grandparents about it all. Remembering that they hadn't been very keen when I started at the zoo, I didn't expect much encouragement in this latest possibility. I wasn't wrong. Grandpa disappeared off to the bowling club with the words: 'Well, you know what they told Mrs Worthington, don't you Neville?'

I laughed. 'No, Grandpa, what was that?'

'Don't put your daughter on the stage,' he said meaningfully, and closed the front door behind him.

After supper, during which Grandma tried to remember all the Victorian music hall turns who'd come to a sticky end (there were quite a few), I tried to think the whole thing over.

I quite liked Pepi and the animals, despite a doubt or two about Diane the monkey. I reckoned I could be happy with them. At the zoo I was still getting new experience of animals, but I didn't want to stay there for ever, and opportunities to change were few and far between, and promotion to the very top a hit-and-miss business. In addition, I was very drawn to the thought of life in variety. In those days, before television and nude shows largely killed it off, variety was still going strong and a major part of the entertainment scene. On top of it all, the money was really good.

I made up my mind: I would take the job. Grandma and Grandpa had gone to bed so would get the bad news in the morning. Meanwhile I rang Blackburn, where I was pretty sure my decision would be greeted as good news.

Tom came to the phone. I explained what had happened. 'By heck, Neville', he said, 'do you mean we'll have a star in the family? I'll go and get your mum.'

She was as pleased as Tom was. 'I always told you there was a lucky break round the corner,' she said. 'I'm sure it's the right thing for you and we both wish you all the very best.' With that she rang off.

As I went upstairs one small cloud was gathering over my happiness. What would the Curator say in the morning when I went to hand in my notice? When morning came the cloud had reached storm proportions. That and the way Grandma and Grandpa took the news didn't make the daily bacon and eggs a very jovial affair.

When I got to the zoo, and went to knock on the Curator's door, I suddenly got cold feet. Had I made the right decision? Would I be letting them down at the zoo? I retreated down the corridor, went out into Bank Hey Street, bought a packet of Players (I didn't smoke much, but I really needed one then), and walked round the block puffing away, coughing, and trying to think straight. I finally thought: it's no good. I've got to face him.

So, back to the zoo, and this time I didn't hesitate. I went straight in to the Curator and got rid of my message with the sort of urgency you would lob an unexploded bomb out of the window.

He sat back. There was no sign of reaction in his face. He was dressed as he always was, in his pin-stripe chief accountant's rig. At last he spoke, after what seemed an age, and what he said was exactly what you might expect from someone who didn't just *look* like an accountant.

'Well, Neville', he said, 'I can't really stand in your way. And, with that sort of money involved, I couldn't promise you a rise that would come anywhere near it.'

He lowered his spectacles and peered at me in the first show of concern about me rather than the finances involved. 'I hope you know what you're doing.'

I made suitable noises.

'Well, as long as you're sure. As far as the zoo's concerned we'll be sorry to lose you.' He reached for some paperwork on his desk, which seemed to be a sign for me to go. Why had I worried that there might be a storm?

I closed the door behind me after a final promise to put my notice in writing, and thought: Well, that's over. Now all I've got to do is to see Pepi's act.

That evening I presented my signed card at Feldman's Theatre. I sat in the stalls of the little theatre, taken in, as ever, by the atmosphere, but realizing with pleasure that, assuming I liked what I saw that evening, I would soon be on the inside of the gilt and plush, the blare of brass and the scent of greasepaint; inside that magic world, one with the stand-up comedians, the trampolinists, the uni-cyclists, the song-and-dance specialists and the chorus high-kickers. I would have only a small part, but I didn't care.

After what seemed an eternity of other acts, the programme number indicating Pepino And His Miniature Circus went up in the frame at the side of the stage, the band struck up 'The Pony Gallop' and I thought, 'Here we go.' The curtain rose, and there on stage were Pepi and Flicky the pony. But what a change! Pepi was made up as a clown, with bulbous red nose, red wig and loud check suit. Flicky was dolled up to the nines and nearly as unrecognizable in ostrich plumes. They were in the middle of a miniature circus ring. Just the sight of them brought spontaneous applause. Then Flicky went into her routine, Pepi controlling her with his long whip, of which he was an absolute master, never hurting her, but just touching her with a slight flick to tell her to change legs, or trot, or whatever. All the time Pepi kept up a running commentary of wisecracks, and encouragement for the little pony. The audience loved it.

Next, on came one of the little dogs, Ginger – who was

to play quite a significant role in my life later on; he ran in and out of Flicky's legs as she went round the ring until it was time for Flicky to take a carrot from Pepi. 'Want your rations?' I heard him say at this point, for the first time in hundreds. Then Flicky took her bow to tremendous applause. Stagehands now came on and

placed hurdles in each quarter of the ring, followed by Peggy the Great Dane, looking beautiful and wearing a sort of harness and saddle. She went through a routine with Pepi. Next to appear was Mike, dressed in the satin trousers and circus shirt that I realized I would have to wear. I looked intently, trying to memorize everything he did. With him was Diane the monkey, in a sort of jockey-cap and outfit; after a bow to the audience, she went on to Peggy's back. The drums rolled, and the music changed to a fast tarantella, and to the astonishment of everyone in the audience, including me, there were Peggy and Diane careering round the ring, and clearing the hurdles in their own form of the Grand National. Finally, when at top speed, Pepi cracked his whip: this was the signal for Diane to let go of Peggy's harness, and sail through the air into the arms of Mike, who was waiting to catch her. More thunderous applause; all round me I could feel the obvious delight of the audience.

But if they thought this was spectacular, it was nothing to the finale. All the little dogs came on, and once more the music sped up to breakneck pace as they careered round the top of the ring in one direction – all except Ginger. He was released from the opposite side and charged round on a collision course until, at the very last second, he became airborne, and leapt over the rest of the troupe one by one. The noise and spectacle made the whole thing quite astonishing. The dogs all wore bells and small Union Jacks, and round and round they went, Ginger never failing to leap at the right moment and clear the lot of them. It was a knockout. The audience cheered and clapped and stamped as the curtain came down, and I sat back knowing that there was not the slightest doubt remaining about my immediate future.

The following Monday at eight o'clock I walked the short distance from my grandparents' house to the paddock near the railway sidings. Mike was already there and at work cleaning out the van. Flicky was tethered on a long rein to a post, munching grass. The monkeys were in their cages but outside in the fresh air, and Peggy was exercising herself, sniffing away at the perimeter of the field.

Pepino himself was not to be seen, but Mike was obviously used to organizing – if that's not too strong a word – the running of the outfit in his own leisurely way. Not far from the van he had a small primus going with a great iron pan of meat cooking for the dogs. I looked into it and thought: 'I suppose he knows what he's doing.' At the rate things were going in the iron pan it looked as if the dogs might eventually be suffering from night-starvation.

I approached him, and he took the chance to rest on his broom and light up a Sweet Afton. 'What do you want me to do, Mike?' I asked.

He blew a long cloud of smoke and considered the question. Eventually, with a friendly grin, he said: 'Nothing, Neville, nothing at all.'

'Well,' I thought, 'that figures.' It wasn't a very encouraging start.

But Mike hadn't finished. He stubbed out his cigarette, carefully put his broom aside, motioned me to come and sit on the step of the van, and launched into another of his conversational rambles that took the best part of an hour. During this time I got two separate tips for the Grand National direct 'and no messin' from the famous O'Brien stables in Co. Tipperary, both of them certainties, which I took to mean that the Grand National that year would result in a dead heat. Or perhaps I just hadn't understood. I was also given the names of three pubs in and around Liverpool which not only stayed open after hours ('they closes, Neville…but they don't shut…get my meaning? Eh?' Nudge, nudge) but also served the genuine Guinness from Dublin, and not 'that terrible gnat's water from Park Royal'. In addition I was given assorted character readings of at least half a dozen theatrical landladies up and down the country whom I should avoid at all costs. Their vices ranged from undercooking spuds to overcharging for baths. Each and every one was a 'terrible, terrible woman'.

In between all this I managed to piece together some kind of picture of what I was meant to do. Rendered down and shorn of the frequent variations on 'Do you get my drift, Neville?' and 'You understand what I'm driving at', it came to something like this: 'We've got a free week here in Blackpool before we're on the road again…as I understand from himself I'm to see you through this and your first week in the theatre…we're playing Bradford, incidentally...but this week all you need do is get to know the animals in your own way and see what I do in the way of looking after them...and if you want to know anything just ask... then next week you can watch me in the theatre and weigh off all the cues and so on...'

At last he got off the step and turned with an encouraging grin: 'You'll soon know the ropes.' Then he ambled over to the brew of dog's meat. While we'd been talking, or, more accurately, Mike had been talking, it had just managed to get to the point of adding a strange, gamey scent to the spring freshness.

So I was left to get on with it, gradually doing more and more as the week went by, and eventually, with only token opposition from Mike, taking charge of the feeding. The first thing I did was to try and speed up the cooking of the dog food. It struck me that for this week at least, with a perfectly good gas cooker at home only ten minutes away, why bother with a boy scout primus? I asked my grandmother if she minded my bringing back some meat to cook.

She said she didn't, but somehow I don't think she would have been so willing if she'd realized the full extent of what I intended. I brought the entire iron pan back with me one morning, set it on the stove with two burners going, and in no time the house was filled with an aroma which brought my grandmother immediately into the kitchen.

'Whatever are you doing, Neville?' she asked, holding her apron to her nose. I explained. There was a muffled sound of disapproval as she went out quickly, very pointedly shutting the kitchen door. But worse, as far as she was concerned, was to follow. When the meat was cooked (and even I could hardly stand the smell), I poured off the juice and left the house carrying the pan of steaming meat back to the paddock. I caught sight of my grandmother watching, with a look more in sorrow than anger, from the front window as I departed. But I knew there would be hell to pay when I got back, and such is the power of grandmothers over 'boys' of thirty-three, I didn't relish it. Sure enough, when I returned there was a small set-to. I was forcibly reminded that we lived in a 'refined' part of Blackpool; what would the neighbours think of my carrying steaming pans of meat down the street, etc., etc. I didn't mind. It was worth it not to have to use the primus.

The week passed pleasantly enough apart from this minor drama. I had the afternoons off and used to go fishing off the end of Central Pier, which made a great change from afternoons spent in the confines of the zoo with not many visitors. I was due back at the paddock at 5 p.m. to let the dogs out for a run, and soon I was being greeted by whinnyings, yelps and barks, just as Pepi was welcomed, as if to say, from inside the van, 'Here's our new friend.' Peggy, who was such a gentle, big creature, I soon made friends with. The little dogs needed an eye keeping on them. I even made headway with Diane the monkey. Pepi kept more or less in the background. He knew I had to make my own relationship with the animals. But when he did appear he was sure to give a word of encouragement. 'That's the style, Neville,' he would say, trying not to look as if he was checking on progress.

Sunday, and time to start life on the boards in earnest, came soon enough. Whether by accident or design, Mike had by now made sure I was at ease with all the animals and was able to look after their exercise, feeding and general welfare. He, Pepi and I met at 6.30 a.m. for the journey to Bradford. Olga packed us up with three lots of sandwiches in greaseproof paper. The animals were all ready in the van, and on top of the cab were all the props, the sections of the ring, the hurdles and so on. I, to suit a new venture, had brought with me something old and something new. The old was my 'pusser's' (naval issue) green suitcase that had travelled many thousands of miles with me during the war, and still bore a naval label on it: 'Keyham Barracks (Devonport) to Blackpool. Delivered Luggage 1s.7d.' The new was a raincoat to smarten up my image.

So we left. Blackpool was soon behind us, and as we

drove along the little lanes across the Lancashire fells
(Pepi never took the main roads, but always planned his
route so that he could find the best stopping places and let
the animals out for a break) I thought, 'This is the life.' I
was in the back with the animals, because there was only
room for two in the cab, but this didn't lessen the sense of
adventure just like leaving harbour for yet another
voyage. Preston, Blackburn, Burnley went by, no more
than mill chimneys and smudges of smoke in the
distance; we reached the West Riding moors, and in the
afternoon were coasting through the outskirts of Bradford.

Just before 5 p.m. we pulled up at the stage door of the
Palace Theatre. After we'd seen to the animals, Pepi went
in and saw the stage manager. With him he had a sheaf of
band parts. These were the parts for his particular pieces
of music, which would be rehearsed the following
morning; by music hall tradition, first to lay band parts
on the stage in front of the footlights on the Monday
morning would be first to rehearse, and so on in order.
He brought up the subject of digs with the stage
manager, and here was where my first taste of the
not-so-plush side of the bright lights came in. There were
digs for Pepi and Mike, but none for me.

The stage manager had expected only two human
beings with the animals and had made arrangements
accordingly. All he could offer me was a spare dressing
room. It wasn't exactly the Ritz. I was meant to sleep on
the floor and for blankets there were worn-out stage
drapes. And for washing and shaving a single brass cold
tap at the end of the dressing room corridor. So this was
showbiz!

Mike tried to jolly me along. 'You don't need to worry
Neville,' he said, and pulled a sour face. 'You remember
those landladies I was telling you about? Well, we've got
one of them tonight.'

I didn't really believe him, but it was a nice gesture.
Eventually Pepi and Mike went off to their digs and I
took more practical steps to cheer myself up. I had a few
pints of Tetley's Ale and then found a fish and chip shop.

It wasn't a patch on the family establishment in Black-burn; I, let alone Tom, could have given them a few free tips on battering and frying. But it had to do. Like the bed on the dresing room floor, it was the best there was. I went to sleep thinking, 'Best to start the hard way.' But I wasn't very convinced.

Yet by the morning the romance-of-the-theatre idea was back with me. I exercised the little dogs on a piece of waste ground, and Mike turned up shortly to get them ready for rehearsals. He was full of the doings of 'the terrible woman'. 'I'll not last a week there. You see if I don't get something better on my own. I'll bet you had a better night than we did.'

So I offered to swap him the dressing room floor. At which he quickly changed the subject.

After Mike had taken the animals over and seen to their getting to the theatre, I went in to watch the rehearsal. It was the first of many Mondays spent like this, but on this first day I had to watch carefully, just as I watched every show that week, noting the cues, the change of music, the precise moment that Mike brought Diane on for her bow. I watched how the dogs were dispersed, what happened to Peggy when she went off stage; there were a score of things to note and remember.

Other parts of the day also set the new pattern of my life: a pint and a sandwich with Pepi at lunchtime, then in the afternoon sometimes the cinema, sometimes a game of snooker. Pepi had a great eye for this and long before I'd sunk more than two or three reds, he would be on the pink and black.

'Clear the board,' he would say, 'no trouble. Going to give in Neville?' There was no clowning here.

Children used to wait at the stage door offering to walk the dogs. If they looked O.K. we willingly took them up on the offer. Every night I saw Pepi's extraordinary transformation taking place. Between houses, he became even more grotesque. He used to take off his bulbous red nose – that and nothing more – before we slipped up to the Pig and Whistle (the circle bar) for a quick pint. Back to the dressing room, and in no time the call boy would be knocking at the door: 'Mr Pepino, ten minutes.'

That week went by all too quickly in a blur of impressions, and all the time the show was on I was trying to anticipate Mike's every entrance, movement and exit. Saturday night came, and my last dummy run was over. Next time Pepino's Miniature Circus was in action, I'd be up there for real.

The following morning we said cheerio to Mike. 'Don't forget what I said about them landladies, Neville,' he said as we dropped him off at Forster Square Station. And with a wave he was gone. I climbed into his seat in the van with Pepi. I was on my own now.

The next booking was down south, in Sheerness. We left Bradford, and once again taking the narrow country lanes, we made our way over the bleak Peak District passes (it was long before motorways) and across the middle of England. Pepi chatted away, but most of the time I was thinking: shall I be able to catch Diane when she leaves Peggy's back? What happens if she sails through the air, and I miss her? What if she took it into her head to take a dive into the orchestra instead...?

When we did reach Sheerness there was enough to take my mind off whether the act was going to work or not. Not only were there no digs for me once again, but the theatre hadn't even a spare dressing room. I had to sleep in the van with the animals. Luxury, in the form of bigger theatres where the animals would be accommodated inside and there would be proper theatrical digs for me, was still in the future.

But it worked out quite well: an atmosphere of kerosene, hay and animals in general saw me off to sleep. Certainly I could think of worse anaesthetics, and I really quite enjoyed the feeling that should anything happen I was there on the spot to look after Flicky, Peggy and Co. Next morning my thoughts were back on how I would shape on my stage début. But, when the time came to move the animals into the theatre, Diane did her best to take my mind off the butterflies that were shifting around in my stomach. She bit me as I took her from the van.

The first house was due to begin at 6 p.m. I had the

animals all ready in good time: Ginger stage right, Peggy stage left. Diane, looking unrepentant, stage left, secured and warming her backside on a radiator where she had a good chance of making a grab for unwary chorus girls – she was very fond of chorus girls, was Diane.

Pepi seemed to take ages turning up, and I was already in my satin trousers and circus shirt, sitting jittery and looking every minute at my watch. He, seasoned professional that he was, timed his arrival exactly to give him the precise amount of time to make up, and sat in the dressing room in front of the electric bulbs round the mirror chatting unconcernedly as he reached in leisurely fashion for the various Leichner greasepaint sticks, applied the spirit gum, and stared appraisingly from time to time at his changing reflection. He seemed to be taking this night like every night that had ever been. But just before we went on he gave me a pat on the arm. 'Good luck, Neville,' he said.

I heard the applause for the comedian as he came off – the act preceding ours always had to be a front-cloth spot so that behind it the stagehands could get the ring ready for us on the main part of the stage. Then I heard the 'Pony Gallop' strike up, more Oohs and Ahs from the audience, and, from the wings, saw Pepi going smoothly and expertly through his routine with Flicky... then Peggy was on ... then I had Diane out of her cage and ready ... waited for the cue ... and we were on. Blinding light was my first impression; I was just able to see the musical director and his baton, but of the audience beyond the footlights I couldn't see further than Row C. Then I heard the applause for us as I walked Diane down to the footlights, held her hand, said 'Take a bow, Diane', and helped her into the saddle on Peggy's back. No time for butterflies. So far, so good, and back into the wings.

Count the number of jumps she did on Peggy's back, to wild applause ... five ... six ... we're on again ... see Pepi crack his whip ... and Diane soaring through the air towards the lighting grid... lose her for a panic split-second in the lights ... then I've got her, caught in mid-air, and, prepared by a warning from Mike, managed to avoid her proving she was the main artiste by biting me. Down to the footlights again, quick bow, rush off, tie her to a radiator, and round to the other side to fix the Union Jacks and handbells on the small dogs.

So it went on, till the stagehands were helping me catch the little dogs as they came off into the wings, and it was all over until the second house. I took the dogs for a bit of exercise in between houses, saw Flicky had enough hay to munch, managed a drink myself and had time to watch some of the other acts, feeling somehow possessive, and that I was part of the whole business. The second house went off as well as the first, and I went to bed that night as part of the troupe, feeling pleased and elated, the more so because Pepi and I had had a final drink, with a 'Well done, Neville. That was all right, wasn't it?' The pint tasted extra good.

The routine at Sheerness became my life, and all the times we were on stage, apart from that first night, have blurred into one. Occasionally there was a panic which broke the routine, and one occurred that first week in Sheerness. Diane escaped from her cage, fortunately well before the performance.

It was lucky that Pepi himself, for some reason, happened to be in the theatre. The first we knew about it was a phone call to the stage door. 'One of your monkeys,' said an anonymous voice, 'is up a lamppost on the promenade.'

Pepi, from being a clown, turned instantly into a man of action. 'Come on Neville. Get Peggy and get the saddle and harness on. It's the only way we'll get her back.'

Out of the stage door we went, Peggy wondering what the fuss was about, and loping gently along in between us. We reached the promenade where Diane had gathered a bigger audience than we normally managed in the theatre.

'Hello Diane,' said Pepi, producing an onion from the stock of titbits he always carried in his pockets. For a moment Diane took no notice and continued swinging about and generally showing off. Then she looked down again. The onion won the battle with her artistic temperament. She slid down the lamppost and on to Peggy's back, and, for all the world like Lester Piggott riding a winner into the unsaddling enclosure, proudly rode back in the saddle to the theatre.

'Well,' said Pepi, when she was safely back in her cage, 'I suppose it got us some publicity.'

The theatres we played in those final boom days of that very British form of entertainment were as varied as variety itself. There were theatres so small that they had no scene docks to provide a means of entrance for Flicky. She was too big to negotiate the stage door, so gave the audience an extra treat by making her second house exit, ostrich plumes and all, via the centre aisle and front of the house. There were theatres so dilapidated, damp and bleak that Pepi would come into his dressing room to find that mice had eaten into his jacket and made a fine meal of the titbits in his pockets. Some of the theatres were oddly constructed like the City Varieties Theatre,

Leeds, well known today on television for *The Good Old Days*. The stage there is tiny, and has no access round the back between wings. Whenever we worked there the ring had to be reduced to a semi-circle, Ginger's spectacular leaping had to be cut, and there were problems getting the animals all entering stage right. Still, the audience was none the wiser, and however reduced the act was we always went down well in Leeds.

At the other end of the scale were the great theatres on the Moss Empires circuit. Nothing put Pepi into a better humour than a letter from his agent saying we were to appear in Manchester, Liverpool or Nottingham, or one of the other theatres on this famous circuit. I always knew when he came into the bar with a letter from his agent in his hand whether the next booking was a good one or not. If he took the light ale I'd lined up for him and said with a great smile, 'Don't know how we can drink this stuff, Neville', I knew it was what he called the Whisky and Soda Circuit the following week, Moss Empires – in contrast to our usual Light Ale Circuit.

One reason for celebration was that we were on a percentage of what was nearly always good business, which meant a bonus for me. Another was that the theatres were large and well run, with excellent dressing room accommodation. Even the animals got their own rooms instead of having to sleep in the van.

Most of all, Moss Empires represented the Big Time. Pepi was always a foot taller at the prospect of seeing his name on the same bill as Big Bill Campbell and his band, Max Bygraves, already a famous singer and comedian, and Robb Wilton, the quavery-voiced comedian with his famous monologues about the fire station ('Oh, you're reporting a fire are you? Well try and keep it going till we get there') and his catch-phrase, 'The day war broke out, the wife said to me...'

I used to love watching Robb Wilton working, a real music-hall star who had you in stitches backstage however many times you'd heard him before. I still remember the lines that made the audiences roar: '...so the wife said, "If you're standing there on the cliffs of

Dover, and Hitler invades...how are you going to know it's Hitler?" So I said..."Well...I've got a tongue in me head, haven't I?"'

The real Mrs Robb Wilton somehow seemed a bit like the mythical wife portrayed in the sketches. She sat knitting in the dressing room while her husband was out front, and as soon as he was off she drove him back to his hotel. They were never known to hang around and join the rest of us for a drink.

By contrast, we used to see a lot of Max Wall, who liked a glass of Guinness, and whenever we were on the same bill made a great fuss of the animals. Max Wall, to my mind, is one of the greatest comedians ever to grace the stage, and he was also in the true music-hall tradition. Before the war he had been a dancer appearing all over Europe and on the same bill as the great Grock, from whom he obviously learned a great deal. But he didn't become a comedian until the war, when he was in the R.A.F. in Blackpool – who knows, he may have been one of the scores of R.A.F. men who used to drink in the same bar as I did when I went on leave.

When the American style of one-line gag and wisecrack was being taken as a pattern for comedians over here it was marvellous to hear Max Wall. He built his act, developed characters, and wasn't afraid of using the English language, as well as having his own twists to traditional jokes: 'Well, ladies and gentlemen, I saw this fly. You know the kind of fly I mean...the kind of fly you look at, and you wonder...what part does this tiny creature play in this great Universe of ours...? Well this fly...this fly landed in Mabel's soup...she had to make a great production of it, of course...she shouted "Waiter! There's a fly in my soup...Remove this insect!"...so the waiter came along and threw me down two flights of stairs...'

His act ended with the most hilarious piece of mime and illusion I've ever seen. He would play a piano with the piano stool too far from the instrument, but instead of moving either stool or piano, Max Wall managed to make his arms appear a foot longer than they really were.

It was a marvellous end to an inspired beginning: 'Ladies and gentlemen...I will now render...remembering that "to rend" means "to tear apart"...Rachmaninov's Prelude in C Sharp Minor...with the aid of an A.A. Guide and a spirit-level...' In the wings we were doubled up.

Off-stage Max Wall was kindness itself, and, as far as Pepi's act went, he made an astonishing and quite unique gesture. Plenty of performers took a shine to our animals, but none of them went as far as Max Wall in showing what they really thought. He particularly liked Peggy the Great Dane, and always came to give her a pat and a stroke when we were rehearsing or getting ready. One day he turned up to the theatre with a box in gift wrapping and left it at the stage door for Pepi. In it there was a handsome brass neckpiece, engraved: 'To Peggy With Love From Max Wall.' From then on she never went on stage without it.

Not long afterwards the animals came in for more adulation while we were playing a Moss Empires theatre. We were at the Palace, Manchester, and on the same bill as Laurel and Hardy. These two Hollywood comedians had by then given up making the films which now, half a century later, get such wide T.V. exposure, and had come to do a British variety tour.

My mother had so often taken me to see them on the screen when I was a child that I greatly looked forward to meeting these comic heroes. Predictably, perhaps, they were far more sensible and sober when I actually met them than they had ever appeared on the receiving end of custard pies. But if I was a bit disappointed, the animals certainly weren't.

Mrs Hardy was a great animal lover, and kept a special table in the dressing room with bon-bons, sweetmeats and French pastries on it. She struck up an immediate friendship with all the animals in our act. She referred to them as 'my little loved ones', and used to say to me, 'Now Neville, come in any time you want, and don't be afraid to take as many of these as you want for dear Peggy and all the rest of those sweet creatures.'

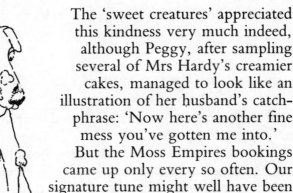

The 'sweet creatures' appreciated this kindness very much indeed, although Peggy, after sampling several of Mrs Hardy's creamier cakes, managed to look like an illustration of her husband's catchphrase: 'Now here's another fine mess you've gotten me into.'

But the Moss Empires bookings came up only every so often. Our signature tune might well have been an echo of one of Max Wall's own songs: 'Big Time, Small Time, 'What's It Matter?' We played end-of-the-pier shows; we slept on bomb sites when playing London theatres such as Collins's Music Hall in Islington; when we were playing the Woolwich Empire we slept in the East India Dock Road and people brought fish and chips to the van with a generosity I shall never forget; we played revue and on cinema bills, filling in with the Mighty Wurlitzer organ in between the feature films; we even joined a tenting circus for two weeks in North Wales. Here I doubled the size of my biceps because, like everyone else from the Strong Man down, we had to help heave the Big Top up and dismantle it every night before moving on the next day. Blackpool now seemed a different world and the nearest we had ever come to it was when we had a booking in Blackburn and managed a surprise visit to my mother.

In all the time I'd been with Pepi this was the first time we'd managed a booking in Blackburn. I'd kept in touch with my mother, sending her regular picture postcards of the places we were playing, and I'd had letters back from her and Tom giving what news there was. I knew that the fish shop was thriving, but that Tom hadn't been in too good health. When Pepsi bustled in one day with the news, we were in the middle of an exhausting week at the Ciné

Variety, East Ham, involving half a dozen shows a day starting at 10 a.m. This was really the far end of the scale from Moss Empires. It was hardly even the Light Ale Circuit, more like Flat Beer. But Pepi's news was a tonic.

'By God, Pepi,' I said, 'this is home cooking for a week!'

His eyebrows shot up. 'Fish and chips, and those Bulldogs you keep on about?'

'Not only that,' I said, 'you'll get the best Lancashire hot pot in the world.'

And so it proved. Cooking apart, I could hardly wait for the last house on Saturday night so we could load up and get ready to go back north and see my mother for the first time in ages. I rang to tell her and she was thrilled. When we arrived, there was a welcome, not only for Pepi and me but for the animals, who got an unexpected break.

'Where are the animals, then?' said my mother, after we'd been indoors for half an hour dealing with an enormous spread of tea and plum bread and cheese, and telling all our news. Pepi explained they were still in the van.

'Well, bring them out,' said Mum, 'it's the least you can do. I've heard so much about them, anyway, I think I'll know them on sight.'

So out to the van we went, and within a few minutes there was one of the strangest sights Blackburn had seen for a long time: a pony grazing in a small back garden with a Great Dane, and inside the living room half a dozen other dogs and two monkeys!

The rest of the week was a bit like that. Something quite out of the ordinary, out of the normal routine; for me it was almost like a holiday to spend some time with Mum – who, with Tom, came to see the show for the first time.

But the next week was back to routine. Pepi's agent had a genius for booking us at alternate ends of the country in alternate weeks, and this was no exception. We'd driven from London to Blackburn. Now it was back to London again, this time the Camberwell Palace.

We accepted this sort of thing as part of the life we led, yet I sometimes wished things could be better organized, and when we waved goodbye to Mum and Tom on the Sunday morning I felt out of sorts not just because I was leaving home.

One of the hazards of playing the Camberwell Palace during the summer was that there was a jam factory close by, and jam factories meant wasps, in droning squadrons. They infested the dressing rooms, bombed in through every available door and window, and generally made life a trial for us, as well as being dangerous when the animals were on stage: one sting could have brought disaster. Whether a wasp was responsible or not I don't know, but one afternoon following a matinée, Ginger got into a fight. It wasn't his style at all, because he was normally a very friendly little animal. But, for whatever reason, there was a great dust-up between the dogs. Ginger came off worst, and had his neck bitten.

After retrieving him, I had to find out where he could be treated. 'Sister Mabel's Dispensary run by the R.S.P.C.A.,' said the stage manager, and gave me directions. I took Ginger along, and it immediately struck me how orderly everything was in the little clinic, how efficient the treatment was, and how caring, and what little fuss there was. It was a new look for me at yet another approach to animals, despite the number of times at the zoo when I had been involved in the vet's treatment of, for example, a leopard having a tooth out, or a tigress in labour. This was something very different, and I can't really explain why I was so impressed.

A Major Breckie cleaned up Ginger's wound, while the dog, calm now, sat patiently. Then the wound was dressed, and he was given a reassuring pat which earned a tail wag. On an impulse, I said to the Major, 'How do you join the R.S.P.C.A.?'

'Well,' he said, in a clipped ex-Army tone 'bit difficult to say. There are several ways. Best thing is to apply to our Headquarters in Jermyn Street.'

I thought about it on the way back to the theatre. I wasn't unhappy with Pepi, despite the up-sticks-and-away aspect of life with the Miniature Circus. And I loved Peggy, Flicky and the rest. Yet, in a strange way, going to the little R.S.P.C.A. clinic had affected me. It seemed to represent something more important than simply looking after animals either for a stage act or in a zoo.

Lying in my bunk in the van that night under the kerosene lamp, with various dog snores and snuffles all round me – it was yet another bomb-site week – I made up my mind to try my luck with the R.S.P.C.A. The following morning, after I had seen to the animals, I took a tram from Camberwell Green to Victoria, and walked from Vauxhall Bridge Road through St James's Park to Jermyn Street. Eventually, after a lot of persuasion of doorkeepers, I managed to see Mr Rogers, the clinic superintendent. In his office I began to wonder whether I had done the right thing. I was made to feel like an enemy dragged in for interrogation.

'Why do you want to leave what you're doing? You know, don't you, that the R.S.P.C.A.'s policy is dead against circuses and performing animals? What sort of act are you in?' And so on.

I tried as best I could to say that animals were my life, and that I liked them. But it didn't sound very convincing. Then he opened a drawer, pulled out some forms, and said, 'Well, we've no vacancies at the moment, but you might as well fill in these forms.'

I spent five minutes answering questions about Experience With Animals, For How Long? and Reasons for Wishing to Join the R.S.P.C.A.

Mr Rogers glanced through what I'd written.

'Hm. Well, Mr Whittaker, we'll let you know. It may be a week or two. But don't pin any hopes on it.

He shook hands managing at the same time to convey that my particular hand belonged to an ogre, and was tainted with making money out of the performance of animals. I walked out feeling a bit down, but cheered up in the summer sunshine. There was the next performance to think about, and I had to take Ginger back to the clinic beforehand. Perhaps the R.S.P.C.A. would reply, perhaps they wouldn't. It was like one of Max Wall's songs: 'Big Time, Small Time, What's It Matter?'

6

A New Life

A Monday morning in the autumn of 1951. We were playing the Theatre Royal, Hanley, in the Potteries. I put out the sheet music around the orchestra pit for the ten o'clock band call. One or two musicians were already there giving a semblance of life to the empty auditorium, and backstage there were the usual thumps and shouts from stage carpenters, a hurrying figure or so, and the stage manager representing the spirit of It'll Be All Right On The Night. I had already taken the dogs for exercise, and finally the rehearsal, or run-through of the week's bill, got under way. At eleven there was a break. I went down to see if the mail had arrived. I saw that it had, by the envelopes and packets sticking out from the pigeon holes in the cubby-hole by the fireman's office, and, rummaging through WYZ I found a buff envelope addressed to me

I turned it over, and on the back there was a printed picture of a man in uniform gripping the arm of another man who had a stick upheld to hit a dog. It was from the R.S.P.C.A. Pepi came up at that moment and started looking through his box. I think he was waiting to hear from his agent about a new contract. But there was nothing for him.

'No luck,' he said, and, peering over my shoulder, 'How about you?'

'I don't know,' I said, but I thought I might be lucky as I slit the envelope open. When I read what was inside I could hardly believe it, and I just stood looking at it.

'Come on,' said Pepi, 'it's not as bad as all that, is it?'

'It's not,' I said, and handed him the letter.

Pepi read it, and as he did so his face slow-burned into a big grin. What the letter, from the Clinics Department of the R.S.P.C.A. London Headquarters, said was: 'We are pleased to inform you that you have been accepted for work with the Society as a Probationary Clinic Assistant.' Following that were instructions to report to the R.S.P.C.A. Hospital and Convalescent Home, Clarendon Drive, Putney S.W. 15, at 9 a.m. the following Monday.

'Terrific,' said Pepi, 'well done, Neville. It's a good thing we're not on the Light Ale Circuit this week – I can buy you a Scotch!'

'You're on,' I said, feeling on top of the world.

Pepi already knew that I'd applied for the job, and he had agreed that if I got it his wife, Olga, would come up from Blackpool to look after the animals, so there were no worries there, nor, as might have happened with a less big-hearted boss than Pepi, hard feelings that I was to leave the act.

I worked out my week's notice, and it passed uneventfully. The end of the last performance on Saturday came, and from backstage I saw the band packing up, and the last of the audience draining away up the aisles towards the exits. I got the animals back in the van – Peggy, Flicky, Diane and all the dogs – and then returned to the stage, now empty but for one or two stagehands striking odd bits of scenery. The house lights had been turned off, and the safety curtain was down. I looked round; it was a sad moment, a moment of parting with a life I had got used to and liked. I turned, thinking Never Look Back, and made my way out through the stage door for the last time. In front of the theatre the bills with our act on had already been taken down, and, as if we had never existed, those great blue and scarlet block letters in their glass cases announced the following week's attractions to the public, who, I hoped, would not by then have completely forgotten us.

We made an early start the following morning for

London. Pepino's Miniature Circus, give or take Neville Whittaker, was due the following week at the Shepherd's Bush Empire – which was a lucky break because it meant I got free transport near to where I wanted to be.

Neither of us said much on the journey south down the old A5. We stopped once or twice to let the animals out, and by just after ten we were coasting down the Edgware Road towards Hyde Park Corner. Here we drew up. Pepi looked across at me as he put the handbrake on.

'Well, Neville,' he said, 'this is it, old lad.' We shook hands without another word. I got out, unlocked the back, and went round the animals, giving each a pat. Goodbye Peggy, cheerio Flicky...Peggy gave a tentative wag of her tail, Flicky stopped munching hay and looked round at me, and the little dogs got up in their boxes and wagged their tails at me. They all knew something unusual was going on. The normal enthusiasm was missing, and I felt a lump in my throat as I closed the door on them. Pepi was waiting by the driver's door. He gave me an embrace, a gesture very much of the theatre, meaning so many things, so many good wishes for the future and remembrance of times past. Then he was gone.

I watched the van until it disappeared, and suddenly Hyde Park Corner seemed a very big and lonely place. It was a strange feeling standing there with my green naval suitcase (still with a 1s.7d. label on it). I had travelled the length of Britain and back again so many times in that van, and realized it represented a kind of security. Now it was gone. Oh well. Now to find Putney.

This I did with directions from a pavement artist outside the underground station. Pausing from his version of the Mona Lisa in chalks, he said: 'Number 14, mate...goes from over there, near Lyons tea shop.' Not long afterwards I was standing at the front door of a rather palatial white house in Clarendon Drive, Putney, with an ornamental pool in the garden: the R.S.P.C.A. Hospital. A pretty girl in a white coat answered my ring at the day bell. I learned later that this was Helen, one of the senior girls at the hospital. I explained who I was, and, more important, that I had nowhere to stay. Could the R.S.P.C.A. help?

Helen was pleasant but brisk. 'That's why you're here on Sunday, is it? We'll see if we can do anything.'

She showed me into the reception room, and left me there to savour its strange atmosphere: an oil cloth on the floor, a desk with a collecting box, R.S.P.C.A. posters on the walls, and, on the left, the entrance to a huge waiting room with chairs all round it. But the feature that really caught the eye was a glass show-case: in it was a weird display of the incredible objects that had been removed from animals over the years: fish-hooks, gall stones, crown corks, chicken bones, even bits of barbed wire. It made quite an impression on me, and I was peering into it when Helen returned.

'Come with me,' she said, and led me out and down some stairs into the basement, past doors marked X-Ray Room, Surgery One, Surgery Two, past rooms which I could see had cages with animals in them, marked Cat Ward One, Dog Ward Two and so on. We went into the staff kitchen, and while Helen made some tea she said: 'I've been thinking about where you can stay. We've no rooms here for people to live in but you might ask at The Arab Boy – it's just along the Upper Richmond Road. They might have a room that would do you until you get fixed up permanently. But if you don't have any luck there, come back here. We can fix you up on the sofa in the staff room for tonight anyway.'

Well, that was something at least. I'd slept on crowded mess-decks, and in a van full of animals, so a sofa would be no hardship. I thanked her and set off for The Arab Boy. It turned out to be an inspiration on Helen's part, although at first the landlord turned me down flat.

'No,' he said, 'I'm sorry. We've no rooms here.' But then I mentioned the R.S.P.C.A. It was like opening a door and shining a light in.

'Why didn't you say so before?' he said, pulling a pint.

'There's a lady usually comes in on a Sunday, and I'm pretty sure she lets rooms.'

And so it proved. For the next six months my home

was to be in Daylesford Avenue off the Upper Richmond Road, well looked after with marvellous meals and pleasant company. I went to bed that night feeling on top of the world: at last, work that I really wanted with animals, and somewhere permanent to go back to in the evenings. I wanted nothing more.

In the morning I was up bright and early. I ate an enormous breakfast, then set off into the autumn sunshine for the eight-minute walk back to the now familiar white door of the R.S.P.C.A. I pressed the bell again, feeling at the same time both excitement and a twinge of nerves: would I be good enough to get through the training?

Not Helen, this time, but a young man welcomed me in. He showed me straight away down to the staff room to await the call to see the Manager. It reminded me a bit of Joining Routine in the Navy, and, sitting there waiting on the staff-room sofa, I had a smile to myself as I remembered how wily old three-badge sailors used to spin out this process almost indefinitely. But the R.S.P.C.A. was no place for time-wasting, and shortly I was called into the Manager's office.

There behind an impressive desk sat the no less impressive Mr Markham: an enormous man, slightly bald, in his late fifties, who had been a sergeant major in the Marines. He seemed to sense that his physical appearance had a daunting effect, and to offset it smiled the most cordial smile as, with a hand as big as a shovel, he took my application form from me. In fact, as I got to know him over the following months, I came to realize that the only formidable thing about Mr Markham was his efficiency; for the rest he was the kindest of men, and the combination made him a tower of strength round which the entire clinic revolved.

After welcoming me, and filling in a few details, he said finally: 'Well Mr Whittaker, we'd better have you shown round, and you can see what you're in for. If you go back to the staff room, I'll get one of the senior girls to take you over the place; you can settle in, and start properly tomorrow.'

So, eventually, I started my tour of the building, guided by one of the senior staff looking the picture of efficiency in a white coat, with a thermometer in her top pocket and a fob-watch. She could have been a nurse in a human hospital.

We toured the wards, where there were dogs and cats being cared for either before or after operations. Some of them were lively, others did not raise a flicker of interest: this came as a shock to me after being used to circus animals, which were all so full of life. In front of each cage, as on a hospital bed, was clipped a medical history sheet under the name of the pet's owner – all of whom were poor people who could not afford normal veterinary treatment – and also the name of the cat or dog: Brutus, Spot or Olly, Tibby, Kitty or Weeny. It was all very strange to me, and a first indication of how seriously the R.S.P.C.A. took its responsibilities.

Next came the impressive operating theatre (Surgery One, which I had noticed the previous day), with instrument tables, trolleys, adjustable lights, oxygen bottles, sutures, needles and sterilizers. Surgery Two was more like a G.P.'s surgery, with shelves of drugs and an examination table. Then we went downstairs and out of the back door (where I learned that this, and not the front, is where I should have come in) to see the exercise runs, and, back in the building again, a room which bore a sad but necessary notice: 'No Entry. Destruction Room.'

So the day passed, a whirl of impressions, and finally back to Mr Markham, who outlined what I would be doing: learning animal husbandry as well as the drudge-like but necessary cleaning of animal cages and equipment; general post-operative care; work assisting the veterinary surgeons in the theatre; learning how to operate the X-Ray equipment and develop the plates, and a host of other subjects.

'It's a tough six months,' said Mr Markham, 'but if you coped in the Navy, then you ought to be able to cope here.'

The time from then until March passed in a whirl. As

Mr Markham had forecast, it was hard work. But enjoyable. Even the most menial tasks seemed important – and there were plenty of those, from mopping and polishing the parquet floors to rubbing your knuckles raw cleaning blankets and conquering mountains of dog and cat bowls in the huge stone sinks.

For the rest, it was a jumble of impressions: carrying inert dogs to the operating theatre; washing X-Ray plates in hypo and seeing the image gradually form and putting it over a light box; learning bandaging and splints in first aid; the sad business of having to put animals down, leading them down to the basement, knowing they were apprehensive and wondering when they would see their owners again – which was never – giving them a pat or a little kiss to make them feel as happy as possible. Many people whose animals were being put to sleep, or having a major operation, particularly old-age pensioners, would be in tears, and we had to try and ease their distress, even if all we could say was: 'Well, don't worry. You're not to worry. He's in good hands, you know, and if you would like to phone at ten o'clock tomorrow morning, we're certain everything will be all right.'

One incident I found particularly touching, and it has always remained in my mind. We had a spaniel in for a major piece of surgery, the removal of an internal tumour. The dog was anaesthetized and the surgeons began to operate, but they found the growth was so extensive that it was almost inoperable, and the spaniel in fact died under the anaesthetic. The owner phoned at four o'clock, which was the usual time for people to call if their animal was having surgery, and of course she had to be told the bad news. She behaved very calmly and sensibly, and said she would be round at five to take the spaniel's body away. So we cleaned up the poor dog and had it removed to the mortuary, with a blanket over it.

To our surprise, when the owner arrived she had her little daughter with her, a girl of about eleven, and they insisted on both going down to fetch their dead spaniel. We did our best to persuade her not to take the little girl with her, but they wouldn't be put off. It was their pet, and they both wanted to go down. So they went to the mortuary and the little girl simply picked up the dog's head in her arms, kissed its floppy ears, and burst into tears. Then the mother took the dog away, wrapped in the blanket. I wasn't far from tears myself.

Towards the end of the training (by which time, though I didn't know it, a progress report had been marked up by the Manager, and sent up to headquarters) I was considered fit to go and handle a one-man clinic. These clinics were scattered all over London, and I was given a group of three to look after temporarily; at Bow, Bethnal Green and Barnes: which may seem strange, since the first two are in the east end of London, and the third right next to Putney in the south-west.

I really enjoyed this, as I was now on my own for the first time. The clinics were usually a little shop or premises that had been bought by the R.S.P.C.A. You would be taken there from Putney by R.S.P.C.A. ambulance, equipped with a 5-gallon drum of sterile hot water (because there were no facilities for boiling up on the premises), and from there you were on your own, dealing, from the moment you put the 'Open' sign up, with a host of problems, giving first aid and advice, and referring more serious cases to the hour-long visit of the professional vet who came once a day. Apart from that hour with the vet, who was paid per session by the R.S.P.C.A., the clinic was my entire responsibility, and this experience, almost more than anything else, stood me in good stead in later years.

At last my six months were up. That was that, for better or worse. I felt pretty sure I'd done well, but I couldn't be certain. Mr Markham called me in on my final day, and lapsed back into naval language for my benefit. 'Got your draft chit here,' he said, holding a piece of paper in his huge hands. It told me to report to the R.S.P.C.A. Headquarters in Jermyn Street. I set off from Putney that morning, a fresh spring morning with a sprinkle of bright new leaves in the Upper Richmond Road, and as I walked along I turned over the possibilities in my mind. Would I be put permanently in charge at

Bow, Bethnal Green and Barnes? That wouldn't be bad; I'd enjoyed my work there. Would it be another one-man clinic? Would it be the Animal Rescue at Islington? This was a tough spot where I'd also done a stint, and been appalled at the number of pets brought in for destruction for no better reason than the fact that their owners were going on holiday. Or perhaps – I left this thought till last – I would be told I hadn't made the grade. I didn't think I would be told this, but the thought didn't make the journey go any quicker.

I got to the Headquarters in the house donated to the R.S.P.C.A. by Baroness Burdett-Coutts, waited for a time, and at last took the rickety lift to the third floor to see the Clinics Organizer, Mr S. C. White, who was a thickset man in his fifties with a steely eye and a godlike aura. In fact, to the clinics in the outfield he apparently *was* God, with a suitable motto: 'Thou shalt not spend', as he pruned and pared every last unnecessary penny out of their budgets.

On this occasion, however, his mind was not on economy. He came to the point straightaway with me, riveting me across the desk with his eyes. 'Mr Whittaker,' he said, 'we're starting a brand-new venture, and we think that you, with your experience with wild animals, backed up by what you've learned at Putney, could be the man we're looking for...'

My thoughts began to spin away from Bethnal Green and Islington. At the same time I realized my reports from Putney must have been O.K. But what was the new venture?

'I don't know a great deal about it and I haven't any details as yet' (slight dent in the godlike image) 'but I can say we're starting an Animal Hostel at Heathrow Airport. This is to cope with all the wild animals and so forth that are coming through – and if the forecasts are right will be coming through in even bigger numbers in the future – and aren't getting the proper care and attention. Now, how does that strike you?'

How did it strike me? It hit me all of a heap, and I didn't say anything. Which gave Mr White time to furrow his brow and go on talking: 'Well, I know it will be a big challenge, and there's no need for you to make up your mind in the next few seconds. But it ought to appeal – it would have done to me in my younger days – it's something that's never been attempted anywhere in the world before. If you *are* interested, I'll put your name forward at the next full Council Meeting.'

It was an offer I had no wish to refuse, and I said so.

'Fine,' said Mr White, folding up a docket and putting it in a drawer, 'I'll let you know when you're to come up for the meeting.'

His letter arrived a few days later. In the meantime I had a nightmare that the forty members of the R.S.P.C.A. Council burst into roars of laughter at the hilarious mention of the name Whittaker, then all, unanimously, turned their thumbs down.

It wasn't really like that on the actual day of the meeting. Waiting to go into the Council chamber was a bit like a waking nightmare. And once inside, even the portraits of worthy R.S.P.C.A. patrons on the panelled walls seemed to put me on trial. But there was no

Council member who looked remotely like laughing. Instead they asked me a lot of questions about my times at Blackpool Zoo, and my experience with the animals there, and to a lesser extent about the Miniature Circus. There flashed through my mind something that Mr Markham had once said to me at Putney. 'You know,' he said, 'for someone like you who's worked in a zoo and with performing animals to join the R.S.P.C.A. is like an alcoholic joining the Temperance League.'

I just hoped no one on the Council thought the same way. I was sent out, and then recalled. To my immense relief and pleasure I was told I had been appointed as assistant at the Hostel.

7

L-Plates at the Hostel

A September morning in 1952, and I was joining the crowd of rush-hour commuters surging down the stairs into Hammersmith Broadway station. I bought a *Daily Express*, queued for a ticket, then stood on the platform waiting for a Piccadilly Line train, glad that I was going the opposite way to the jam-packed trains which every minute or so shuttled away in the direction of Piccadilly itself, Holborn, and all change for the City.

I had booked to Hounslow West, then the end of the line, and the nearest station to Heathrow Airport. I had an appointment to look round the new hostel before it opened and I started work there later in the month. A train drew in, luxuriously half-empty, and as we rattled away above ground through west London I settled down to read the paper.

On one of the inside pages a heading caught my eye: THIS COMET IS SO SMOOTH, it said. Underneath was a big feature with pictures about Britain's 'Miracle Airliner', the Comet One. It read to me like science fiction. According to the article, the time was only just round the corner when it would be possible to fly from London to Paris with barely time to light up a cigarette and down a cup of coffee. Crossing the Atlantic would take only a matter of three or four hours, with all possible comfort and the smoothest of flight conditions.

We were, said the writer, truly on the threshold of the Jet Era For All. Soon gone would be the days of lumbering round the skies in old piston-engined airliners such as the York, Lancaster and Viking, all conversions from or developments of wartime R.A.F. bombers. Best of all, it concluded, this was an all-British breakthrough, masterminded by de Havilland and powered by Rolls Royce. The Comet was so far ahead of its time as to put American airline development back to the age of the Wright Brothers. It was a lead we must maintain, etc., etc.

The train reached Hounslow West as I was finishing the article. 'I'll take that with a pinch of salt,' I thought as I stepped out on to the platform. I was far readier to accept the reality of the moment in the ungainly, slow shape of a D.C.3, which as I left the station to catch my bus was passing overhead in its descent to the duty runway at Heathrow. They used to say that the D.C.3 – the Old Dakota, also of wartime fame – was powered by a crew of a dozen men secreted under the floorboards and pedalling for all they were worth. I believed in that story rather more than the vision of the future I'd just read.

Next I caught a bus to Hatch Lane. I'd been told to keep an eye out for the Black and Decker factory, get out there, and walk the rest of the way. As we approached I caught sight of what I was really looking for: a new-looking brick building like an aircraft hangar by the side of the A4 main Bath Road, outside the airport perimeter. On it was a great notice: R.S.P.C.A. HOSTEL FOR ANIMALS.

Here it was then, the place I'd thought about continuously since my interview, wondering what it would be like. Now I saw it, all the suspicions of the unknown that had lurked about my mind vanished. It looked good and gave me a shot of confidence. A glass door had a notice saying 'Ring and Enter'. I did so. Inside I was hit by the smell of newness, freshly dried plaster, newly oiled linoleum, and other undefinable scents of a building only just finished. It had that strange untouched atmosphere, and it echoed as an R.S.P.C.A. man came along the corridor to meet me.

He was one of the senior administrative officials from Headquarters put in to get the place started. Later he was replaced by another admin man, Jack Cottis, who was the first real boss of the Hostel. Yet from the word go he acknowledged that I was the expert on wild animals. He freely admitted he knew nothing about them, and turned up for his first day wearing L-Plates on the back and front of his jacket! But this was a little ahead; on the morning I arrived the first admin man was there to show me round.

Off we went, and a thought struck me: why, given the job of designing the very first hostel for animals of its kind in the world, had the architect made it hangar-shaped? It could have been any shape. I suppose because it was to be at Heathrow the architect had decided that it had to be disguised as a traditional airfield building. But it looked more suited to taking Lancaster bombers than crates of monkeys.

Hangar-shaped or not, the interior was spacious and well set out, with big, wide doors to give good access for unloading. On the right were stable doors, creating another illusion: that we were inside a racing stable. There were loose boxes, and next to them a fodder room with galvanized bins for the corn. Close by, all ready, were sacks of bird seed, unopened. Then a deep-freeze to hold meat for the carnivorous animals, and frozen fish for aquatic birds, seals, sea lions, or whatever of that kind came in.

The point was that no one at R.S.P.C.A. Headquarters really knew what *would* be coming in. The Hostel had been designed and everything ordered in advance on inspired (and, as it turned out, quite accurate) guess-work. This was a unique venture, and though its experience had always been largely on the domestic side of the animal world, the R.S.P.C.A. had gone to some trouble to try and forecast what the needs would be. It was like going round an operations centre for a war that had not begun. As we moved along I was more and more impressed at the amount that had been done, and the money that had been spent to ensure that the Hostel lacked for nothing when it eventually opened.

We opened doors, went along corridors, and saw everything. I was not only impressed but getting excited at the prospect of working here. Even the scrapers, brooms and shovels for cleaning out boxes and crates, and the animal rooms of the Hostel itself, were sparkling and new, and, as befitted an inspection, everything was neatly stowed in racks. So too, the kitchen, to the last polished sink and stainless steel knife.

At the far end of the building were thirteen kennels. These were for export dogs not under quarantine, and so were not built to the security standards required by the Ministry of Agriculture and Fisheries. On the opposite corner were a further sixteen kennels, which were fully equipped for quarantine, with double gates, safety gates, and disinfectant pads to prevent infection being carried in or out. Another door was marked Sick Bay. The room was eventually used for quite different purposes, because it was designed to cope with domestic animals, and these were very much in the minority when we started operating.

'Now,' said the senior R.S.P.C.A. man, opening the door leading from the Sick Bay, 'I think you'll like this.' It was the surgery, and was the last word in design and equipment; supplies of medicine, cases of instruments, operating table, X-Ray apparatus, and sun-ray lamps, all stood ready, everything that could possibly have been thought of for the treatment of ailing and injured animals.

Finally we went outside, and I saw the spacious paddock intended for giving horses and larger animals (including many an elephant, as it turned out) a bit of natural space.

'Well, Neville, what do you think of it all?'

'Marvellous,' I said.

'Good. I think we've done as much as possible bearing in mind we've really no idea what problems we might face. Now, if you'll forgive me, there's endless admin still, so I'll leave you to wander about on your own, get the feel of the place as far as possible, and if you've any questions, come and ask me. Then we might have a spot of lunch.'

So I took a turn round the paddock, realizing that a big

task lay ahead, even though I was not in charge. It was one thing to have an idea put to you in an office in Jermyn Street, and quite another to have the extent of it presented to you in one short morning.

At the same time, looking beyond the fence of the paddock, something else struck me. I don't now remember exactly how I had pictured the Hostel in my mind's eye before I ever saw it. What I do remember is that I'd quite definitely assumed that the Airport Hostel for Animals would be sitting right bang in the middle of an airport. But there was no sign of an airport. Where was it? There wasn't an aircraft in sight, nor a hangar (apart from the Hostel building), nor a runway. There was nothing that had anything remotely to do with an airport. Just fields. To anyone who knows the huge complex that Heathrow has grown into over the intervening years, a city in itself sprawling over square mile after square mile, my early picture may be a bit difficult to grasp. But that's how it was.

The R.S.P.C.A. had been given a truly rural site, for which they paid a peppercorn rent of one shilling (5p) a year. Somewhere beyond the horizon were the runways, measured then in hundreds of yards rather than miles, and the half dozen or so wartime huts that did duty for Arrivals, Departures, Transit, Customs, and Immigration, as well as offices for British European Airways (B.E.A.) and British Overseas Airways Corporation (B.O.A.C.) before they were fused into British Airways, and one or two overseas airline offices such as Pan-Am and Air France.

This was Heathrow airport as it was then. It handled mostly the longer foreign flights, while B.E.A. operated a great deal from Northolt, an old Battle of Britain airfield it shared with the R.A.F. a mile or so away. Gatwick was still in the future. We were hidden away in the countryside. Hares ran in the fields. Pheasants nested outside the Hostel windows. A minute or two's walk away there were bags of mushrooms to be had for the picking in the autumn. But if this seems a lyrical setting for the R.S.P.C.A.'s brave new venture it was very much in contrast with the reasons behind it all.

Livestock was coming into Heathrow in a terrible condition: boxes of monkeys, crates of birds dead or dying on arrival, and nothing whatsoever being done about it. The R.S.P.C.A. had carried out a survey, monitoring the arrivals and the casualties, and it was decided that some form of shelter and care simply *had* to be provided. This led to the building of the Hostel at a cost of £21,000, then a considerable sum, particularly for a charity to find from its own funds.

Some examples of what was going on: *en route* from Amsterdam to Karachi, a young lion was unloaded at London Airport and found to be dead. Its metal container was smaller than the overall size of the animal, and had nothing like adequate ventilation. A post-mortem carried out by a veterinary surgeon indicated the animal had died from suffocation and heart failure, most likely through over-exertion as it tried to move in its cramped box, and also because of shock. When a consignment of nearly 4,000 wild Peking robins came in from Hong Kong, no fewer than 700 dead birds were found among the nineteen crates. In this case, veterinary examination showed that the birds had died from pneumonia caused by climatic changes.

These were but two instances – and in this country, at least, the principle that animals are sentient and deserving of consideration had been accepted for many years. The first law giving protection to domestic animals had been on the British statute book since 1822. Year by year the degree of legal protection given to animals was extended beyond that, and the Protection of Animals Act 1911 made it an offence for anyone to 'convey or carry or cause or procure, or, being the owner, permit to be conveyed or carried, any animal in such a manner or position as to cause that animal any unnecessary suffering'.

The problems were not caused simply by flying, and the conditions of airborne travel, however. When creatures arrived at London Airport they came to the freight sheds. In those days that was a pretty accurate description of the draughty, decrepit buildings. Sometimes the freight handlers, with the best of intentions, actually increased the mortality rate by putting animals against the radiators when they should have been kept cold, or by feeding them unsuitable food. No wonder the R.S.P.C.A. saw the idea of a hostel at Heathrow as a top priority.

Not long after my original visit in September 1952 we opened the doors. For staff there was the admin man, myself, and one girl: Jenny Stansfield, the first ever Hostel assistant, a tall, very pretty blonde with blue eyes who caused a sensation among the freight handlers the first time she had to go down to the tarmac. And on every other occasion, come to that. As yet we had no standard uniform, but she wore a starched white coat, and her smartness was exceeded only by the brisk efficiency that went with it.

Small beginnings perhaps, but we got everything in order, including the paperwork, and waited for our first arrivals. We heard there was a cargo of monkeys coming in, and stood by. But a phone call told us that they were flying straight out again without being unloaded.

'What do you bet me we do get monkeys?' I said to Jenny, hoping in fact we would.

'What odds are you offering?'

'Don't know,' I said, not being a betting man.

'Well, what about even money monkeys or birds, a hundred to one crocodiles?'

We laughed and gave up the betting as too complicated. But there was no laughter when our first cargo did arrive a day or so later.

They were two ostriches off a flight from South Africa. One was dead, and we labelled it with a tag that became all too familiar: D.O.A., Dead On Arrival. It was an abbreviation that we ourselves invented out of necessity. For the other ostrich I quickly telephoned for a veterinary surgeon. We had no vet attached to the Hostel so I called in a local man who was also a Ministry of Agriculture and Fisheries vet. He came along and diagnosed respiratory trouble. No doubt it was the first time he had ever treated an ostrich, just as it was the first

time we had ever seen one at close quarters, but his diagnosis proved accurate. For the first time, our animal ambulance went into action, and the ostrich was taken to Putney, where I had so recently come from, to the R.S.P.C.A. Hospital. It was not a happy beginning for us, but at least we had the second ostrich in our hands in time. It recovered from its illness and eventually returned to us before being flown out again to the States. It was some comfort to know that had the Hostel not opened it might also have died.

So that was Panic No. 1. I wondered about the old saying: 'Begin as you mean to go on.' During the next

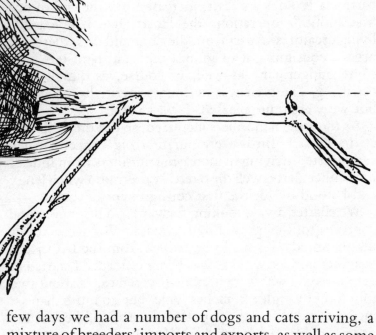

few days we had a number of dogs and cats arriving, a mixture of breeders' imports and exports, as well as some belonging to private individuals going abroad. Yet we knew that these represented only a fraction of the animals coming through Heathrow. It seemed that the airlines had not yet got used to the idea of our existence; not only that, some were reluctant to use us anyway. Despite customs forms and other documents being all ready and waiting, certain airlines (though not our own B.E.A. and B.O.A.C.) at first did not want to be bothered to raise these documents in order to send animals from the freight sheds down to us, as well as having to get a vehicle

101

out, deliver them, and then collect in time for the flights. At the very beginning, we were a bit of a nuisance from the airline point of view.

In fact, B.O.A.C. used to have a hut allocated for dogs and other animals at their training school at Meadowbank a mile or so away. It was run by a man called 'Monkey' Mason. He got his name because he was in charge of the monkey handlers who used to travel on the air freighters. Soon after we opened, it was decided to close this place down, and the flow of animals to us, particularly dogs and cats, increased. By the end of our first month's operations the Hostel had handled 800 living creatures. Apart from the dogs and cats, there had been a consignment of guinea pigs and hamsters, and some budgerigars, as well, of course, as our ill-fated ostriches. The total was nothing to write home about, but we were quite pleased. It was a start.

As the animal numbers increased, so did the problems at the Hostel. Birds were our first big concern. They soon started arriving in increasing numbers from India. I remember all too well the overcast afternoon when Jenny and I stood by for the first consignment of them.

We chatted away, looking forward to a bright oriental contrast to the grey English skies. We were to be disappointed. When a lorry arrived from the B.O.A.C. freighter and I saw what was being unloaded I started to get uneasy. They were hessian-covered cages about two foot long by eighteen inches wide, but no more than six inches deep. I lifted the flap from the front of the first and had a terrible shock. Inside the bamboo cage, crammed and wedged, was a mass of little Indian birds, waxbills, speckled green finches, strawberry finches. But all their brightness was a mockery: many were dead, and others obviously dying. Jenny said nothing, but looked close to tears. I stood shaking my head, unable to believe what I saw.

'Let's have a look at the rest,' I said finally, 'then we'll do what we can for this first batch.'

I hoped against hope that somehow the first cage had been the subject of some accident, that the others would be all right, the birds miraculously alive and chirping away. But barely a sound was coming from the other cages that were by now stacked up in front of us. With each front flap I lifted it was the same story as the first cage, with just a few little survivors staring out from the bamboo slats.

The cages that came in were all of similar construction, made of bamboo, with several bamboo perches inside. Inside, wired to the front, were three or four old Players' cigarette tins, circular in shape and two or three inches deep. These were the sole sources of water for more than three days for up to 300 birds. Needless to say, by the time the freighters reached Heathrow these containers had long since been dried out and piles of dead birds at the front of the cages, all of them desperate to the last for water, were tragic witness to their insufficiency. The birds left India on a Saturday night, and did not reach Heathrow till the following Wednesday. Those that didn't make it to the water and the limited amount of food at the front of the cages dropped to the floor. Others suffocated in the panic, and some fell from their perches through the sheer stress and strain of travel.

This was the first of, sadly, many such consignments. In those early days we had to dispose of thousands of dead and dying Indian finches. We would have felt a bit better if it had been possible to track down the dealers who sent them. But all we ever had by way of origin and identity would be the name of some back-street market in Calcutta or Delhi. What made us even angrier was the fact that we *knew* that it was a regular practice to overfill the cages *deliberately*. The stupid theory was that the more birds that travelled, the more might survive. Overcrowding was never recognized in India as the main reason in itself for the high mortality. This was a strange echo of the methods of human slave traders, who would put a hundred extra negroes in the hold over and above the stated cargo to ensure that on reaching the West Indies or America from Africa, after the dead had been disposed of, the 'correct' number of slaves shown on the ship's manifest would still be delivered to the quayside.

Luckily, life wasn't all dealing with the traffic in finches. We had our lighter moments, as when a white rhino turned up on our doorstep. This huge creature, nearly six foot to the shoulder and of great bulk, is now very rare, although it was plentiful enough in Africa no more than a century ago. This one was in transit to the States. Before he was led in to be the sole guest in our end stable, I had looked up what to feed him. The book said: 'In Southern Africa the White Rhinoceros lives entirely on grass, and there is no evidence of their eating anything else.' There seemed to be no problem, then. We had plenty of grass in the paddock. But, so much for the reference book. It turned out not to be quite so simple. Back in the office there was a signal from the shipper. It said, among other things about this particular rhino: 'He likes spiced buns.'

I read the signal again to make sure there wasn't a mistake in transmission. But no, spiced buns it said, and spiced buns is what it obviously meant. I remembered a strip cartoon that used to appear years ago in a Sunday newspaper. It was called 'Believe It Or Not'. The white rhino would have been a natural.

When I told Jenny she thought I was pulling her leg.

When I finally convinced her we decided we'd better take the Land-Rover and do a tour of the local bread shops. But the citizens of Hillingdon and district didn't seem as partial to spiced buns as our rhino. We could only muster about three dozen.

As we unloaded them, I said: 'These aren't even a mouthful for him. He won't even taste them. We might just as well give him Smarties.'

'You were right,' said Jenny after taking the buns down to the stable, 'he hardly noticed. Gone in a flash. What are we going to do?'

'Search me,' I said. 'We've emptied the shops in Hillingdon, I suppose we'd better go and clean them out in Colnbrook.'

So off we went again in the Land-Rover. I tried one side of the street while Jenny tried the other. When we met back at the Land-Rover I had four or five bags with some genuine spiced buns, but also some baps and bridge rolls – I was getting desperate. But Jenny was empty-handed.

'No luck?' I said, heaving my parcels into the back of the truck.

'No buns,' said Jenny, 'but we might be in luck.'

'Oh, how's that?'

'Well, the last shop I tried didn't seem to know what I was on about when I asked for "spiced buns" and the girl said did I mean hot cross buns because they were taking orders.'

Hot cross buns! This was the answer to a white rhino's prayer. I kicked myself for not thinking of the idea, because it was only two days before Good Friday.

'Of course...I'd forgotten,' I said to Jenny, 'I must be stupid. How many did you order?'

'I didn't order any,' she said. Then added quickly enough to prevent more instant shock showing in my features, 'I just asked for the address of the bakery they get them from.'

'The bakery! You're a genius. Where is it?'

'Staines.'

'Right. Come on, then.' We piled into the Land-Rover and were in the back streets of Staines in no time.

There, sure enough, the bakery was about to launch into its annual production of hot cross buns. After some negotiation and argument about wholesale/retail prices we ordered enough to keep an army of rhinos happy.

Late that evening they were delivered, tray after tray of them, still warm. The white rhino, mooching about his stable, and long ago having disposed of and forgotten my pathetic offering of baps and bridge rolls, perked up at last. By the time he departed on Good Friday even he hadn't quite managed to finish off all we'd ordered, so Jenny and I had the remainder. Six, I think it was. I suppose the moral of the story is that if you're going to entertain a white rhino who is partial to buns, make sure he arrives in Holy Week.

8

The Monkey Trade

When, one day, we had a message to say that a consignment of 800 rhesus monkeys would be coming to us from a flight out of Delhi, we were even more excited than we'd been at the first prospect of Indian birds. These would be the Hostel's first monkeys. It seems astonishing, in view of the intervening years and all that happened, to realize that there was a first time, and that I actually looked forward to the event with great eagerness. In my mind were warm thoughts of old Adam and Eve back in the Tower Zoo, and even little Diane in the Miniature Circus, who used to bite me whenever she could (time heals all flesh wounds). Impatient to greet my newest monkey friends, I took the Land-Rover down to the airport itself when the aircraft was due, and waited on the tarmac for it.

The aircraft appeared at last, somewhere above Staines, losing height towards the duty runway. The approaching sound was a familiar wartime memory: four Rolls-Royce Merlins rasping away. The aircraft, I saw, was a York transport, a civil version of the Lancaster bomber. It sank towards the threshold and I heard the crackle-back as the throttles were chopped. Then the freighter thumped rather heavily on the runway, burning rather more tyre-rubber than necessary, and slewing in the cross-wind. It looked the sort of landing that might just have been acceptable after a trip to Essen and a lot of flak.

But I didn't realize how near the comparison was until

the aircraft had taxied in and I watched the crew emerge. They really did look as if they had come back shot-up from the Ruhr. One by one, captain, second pilot and engineer climbed out. They looked utterly exhausted; saying not a word, they immediately reached for their cigarettes, lit up, and climbed aboard the crew transport.

As soon as I boarded the freighter I realized why. All my eagerness and enthusiastic thoughts of welcome for the monkeys drained from me in a split-second. An unbelievable heat and stench hit me as I reached the cargo door. When I got inside, I found a shambles. At first I couldn't understand the foul atmosphere, with condensation running in streams down every window, down the inside of the fuselage and gathered in filthy pools on the metal floor and by the inner ribs of the aircraft.

Then I saw the cargo, secured with webbing: an interior packed with boxes of monkeys, as well as, further along the fuselage, some dogs and cats, some boxes of birds and even a leopard cub. But what really stopped me in my tracks and completed the picture of what must have been an airborne hell was an eerie, mass whimpering noise that filled the aircraft: the plaintive cries of scores of monkeys clinging with their feet and hands to the chicken-wire of their cages – perched on the bodies of their dead companions.

It was the first cage of Indian finches all over again, only far, far worse, and on a bigger scale. The filth inside the cages was indescribable, and it struck me then that the dead monkeys (they were all destined for an early end anyway for medical purposes in Amsterdam, Brussels, and various places in the United States) were probably the lucky ones. So this was an animal freighter! I was appalled beyond belief, and the more so when I noticed that some of the monkeys that had died had done so unable to move. Their hands and feet were trapped in the battens at the bottom of their cages.

When, later, we arranged to have post-mortems done on a cross-section of these animal victims, no specific cause of death was found, except in one little monkey that might have had a touch of pneumonia. All but this one, young and old, male and female, big and small, died from what the vets quite categorically said was 'stress and strain'. During all the years to follow, this continued to be the prevalent cause of death among the monkeys. Air travel itself, with all its unnatural noise, changes of pressure and temperature, and cramped conditions was the killer.

The eighty boxes of monkeys, ten to a crate, dead or alive, were unloaded and put into our middle stable. During the following hectic and hard-working twenty-four hours we just referred to this as 'The Monkey Stable'. It was a name which stuck for ever. Whatever went in there in later years, they were always in 'The Monkey Stable'.

I said twenty-four hours, and that is literally what I meant. Jenny and I worked all day and all through the night cleaning up the monkeys, and feeding and watering them – those that survived that is. All of them were especially thirsty because they had had nothing but dried peas to eat on the way over. Some of the monkeys who were obviously ailing were removed to our resuscitation cages. At the same time, we saw that the other animals and birds that had come in on this terrible freighter were attended to and made comfortable (in the case of the dogs and cats, before going into quarantine). It was the first of many all-night sessions spent at the Hostel in this way, and a ghastly introduction to what we came to call 'the monkey trade'.

Yet it really *was* only the beginning. Things are said to get worse before they get better, and it was certainly true of the monkey trade. Laboratories in the United States and other countries during the fifties that were manufacturing polio vaccine were crying out for more and more monkeys. The kidneys were used for growing the culture for the vaccine, and, since nature provided only two kidneys per creature, the demand was enormous. It grew more so, as time went on and more laboratories took to manufacturing the vaccine. This, in turn, meant bigger aircraft, so that eventually we had big four-engined American Constellations carrying no fewer than

1,000 monkeys coming in regularly, to be supplemented in later years with Super-Constellations which could transport 1,500.

On board these aircraft there was a high degree of organization. Down the starboard side of the fuselage there would be a row of crates all filled with monkeys stacked three high, stretching from the pilot's door right to the rear of the aircraft. There would be an equivalent stack on the port side, and, down the centre of the aircraft two rows stacked back to back, and, once again, three high. Also on board were hundredweight sacks of peas for feeding, watering cans to fill the water-trays, and a team of monkey handlers to carry out the feeding and watering, and to look after the stock generally *en route*. These 'monkey men' as they were called, were experts and worked really hard for their money, which included a so-called 'mortality' bonus. It was really a *non*-mortality bonus. The fewer monkeys lost, the higher their money.

Despite the care and attention during flight in the big aircraft the monkey deaths didn't stop. It was the same story as before: stress and strain, and bad packaging. Of three shippers of monkeys from India, two were very good with their methods of crating but there was one whose standards were non-existent.

Soon we began to notice something else.

The biggest proportion of casualties per load, sometimes up to 40 per cent of an entire cargo of monkeys, was occurring not on the Constellations but after the introduction of an English-type aircraft called the Hermes. B.O.A.C. became very worried, and we did all we could to try and establish why this new aircraft should be earning such a bad record. At first we put it down simply to accidental causes and the usual stress and strain, but eventually it became clear that there must be some link between the aircraft itself and the high number of monkey deaths whenever one of them flew into Heathrow.

At last, after painstakingly piecing together the clues, we found the cause. The first clue was provided by post-mortem: some of the rhesus monkeys were dying of suffocation. The second clue, which we found after a lot of hard research, was that those monkeys who had suffocated always came from the bottom layers of boxes in the aircraft. We next found, to our horror, that *all* the monkeys that travelled in the bottom layers were dead on arrival.

It was then the turn of the airline to investigate. They discovered that by some accident of design a pocket of stale air built up at the bottom of the fuselage. As the flight went on, the air became virtually all carbon dioxide, and contained hardly any oxygen at all. To counteract this, fans were installed to circulate the air at the lowest level. There was an immediate improvement. At the Hostel we felt pleased that at last we had been able to contribute something positive for the benefit of the monkeys whose only 'crime' was that they had been unlucky enough to be caught.

Of course, we were still unable to do anything about the other main causes of mortality. As time went on the terrible business of the monkey trade continued, ever expanding, so much so that the R.S.P.C.A. had to take on extra Hostel staff to cope with sometimes as many as eight or nine thousand monkeys *a day* coming through. This used to happen when there was a sort of log-jam with the super-freighters. Apart from the aircraft scheduled to come in, others would unexpectedly arrive on the same day because they had been delayed through weather or operational difficulties *en route*. Or perhaps there would be forecasts of fog or bad icing conditions in Canada or the U.S.A., and as many as four freighters each destined to carry a cargo of 1,500 monkeys would delay their take-off until the Met. Office and Flying Control cleared them. And as they sat empty on the tarmac on the north side of Heathrow, other freighters (usually on charter to B.O.A.C.) would be coming in. So the Hostel was literally filled with monkeys. There were boxes of monkeys everywhere, stacked up four crates high, even in our kitchen. The racket at feeding time was unbelievable. In the winter we consumed enough electricity for a small town in an effort to supplement the central heating and keep the temperature equable at about 65 – 70°F. We had a battery of electric fans keeping the warm air moving and controlling the humidity, because monkeys are very chesty creatures. This is their weak spot, and they swiftly start going downhill if conditions are not exactly right.

Sometimes we would have a consignment in for which we had originally entered on the cargo manifest, say, '52 D.O.A.' By the time the consignment left the Hostel for the next leg of its flight the number would perhaps have to be amended to '80 D.O.A.'. Not much of an advertisement, it might be thought, for the Hostel. But we had done everything in our power to look after the survivors properly. And our troubles were not always over even then.

There would be a call from B.O.A.C. to say the freighter was due out again the following morning. The monkeys would be prepared for the journey. The night staff would get up and begin feeding them at 6 a.m. (they were normally fed twice a day, the other time being at 5 p.m.). Their food for the flight was already provided, and this was never touched in the Hostel. Instead, we gave the monkeys English wheat and barley, which was bought in tons at a time and kibbled maize (the Americans call it cracked corn), which helps to give body-warmth. The cages would be given a final clean, fresh sawdust put in after the trays had been disinfected, food-pots and water-tins filled. Everything was made ready. The monkeys looked chirpy after a good night's rest and care, and really had every appearance of being on top form as they left the Hostel, to be driven off in the lorries to the waiting Super-Constellation.

Yet we crossed our fingers as we saw them off, and advisedly so. Not infrequently, within an hour of their leaving us there would be a call from the duty head loader to say that the captain refused to take off until the dead monkeys had been removed from their crates! It always seemed unbelievable. How *could* the captain on his pre-flight inspection have found dead animals when the

entire consignment had left us such a short while ago
looking so lively, so cheerful, and so animated? But there
never was any mistake. We would despatch our ambulance down to the tarmac and do what was required, and
return, thinking frustrating thoughts about the seeming
hopelessness of stopping this baleful business for good
and all.

Yet it went on and on. In the meantime, two
significant events happened to me personally. The first
was when I met a girl called Peg. She ran, stocked and
made clothes for her own dress shop in Hillingdon. We
met at a little club in the village, but it was her dogs that
really brought us together, Barnie and Buster, a lively
pair of bull terriers. Whenever she was there the dogs
made a great fuss of me as I went into the club, so it was
obvious that I had to get to know their dark, attractive
owner. When I did I found we had two great interests in
common: one was animals, which she adored, and the
other, more unusual, was that she came from a music-
hall family, loved variety, and knew the acts of Florrie
Forde, Max Miller and many of the stars of the world I
myself so much admired and had briefly been a part of.
We had plenty to talk about, and in 1955 we got married.

Since then she has not only put up with the odd and
irregular hours we had to work at the Hostel, dictated by
the arriving and departing animals, but many times
helped out there: on one very forgettable occasion Peg
even earned the scars to go with it. I was on night duty
alone as the rest of the Hostel staff were down with 'flu.
A consignment of vultures arrived at 2 a.m. and had to be
uncrated. It was too big a job for me alone, and the only
way I could get help was to ring Peg. She came down and
we got the birds out of their boxes. But we both finished
up in casualty at the local hospital: the vultures had been
too much of a handful and left their claw marks deep
enough to need stitches.

The following year, 1956, brought promotion. I was
appointed Manager of the Hostel. Once again I was
interviewed by the full R.S.P.C.A. Council, and sat in
front of the great baize table being grilled – not least to

my eyes by the portrait of Queen Victoria, who seemed to have an unusually disagreeable look throughout the interview. I felt I was trying to convince her as well as the Council of my fitness to be solely responsible for the animals that were one of the great interests of her life. But if Queen Victoria had the casting vote, I'm for ever grateful to her. The competition was stiff: eleven other candidates (by R.S.P.C.A. rules the post had to be advertised throughout the organization). But I was the only one with direct experience of the Hostel and its problems.

Once again, as on the occasion four years previously, I walked out into the sunshine and took a turn across St James's Park. I couldn't help wishing that there and then, by some miracle, I might run into the white-coated P.D.S.A. man from Blackpool, the man who had loftily turned me down years ago because I had no qualifications...and tell him, with great satisfaction, my news!

Back at the Hostel, however, it was back to reality, quite apart from the realization of an ambition. The Council had been at pains to find out during my interview whether, aside from my practical experience, I knew about all aspects of R.S.P.C.A. policy and thinking, and also that I could cope with the administration. It was just as well, because there was plenty of that. But I never let it get in the way of what I regarded as the most important task: seeing to the animals, and now I was in a better position to do so, seeing what could be done for the plight of the monkeys that travelled by air.

But not all the monkey drama was concerned with the terrible conditions they travelled in when airborne. One incident concerned a large female rhesus monkey who came to be known first as Freda, then as Fearless Freda. For all the wrong reasons she became one of the Hostel's biggest celebrities.

Freda escaped one day through carelessness at the freight sheds. She was being unloaded and suddenly saw her chance. In next to no time she was away, and taking a bout of healthy exercise round the airport. We were alerted and crossed our fingers that she couldn't get out of

Heathrow. We were soon disappointed. Within an hour the telephone was going again.

'R.S.P.C.A.? We've just seen a monkey crossing the Bath Road. We thought you ought to know.'

At least we knew where she was: somewhere on the other side of the A4 from us, where there was a row of semi-detached houses. I went to get Jenny. We got out some monkey-catching nets on 6-foot poles which had just lain in the store since the Hostel opened, but just as we were leaving, the phone rang again.

'R.S.P.C.A.? I spoke to you before. The monkey's just shinned up a drainpipe and it's on the roof of one of the houses.'

Now that *was* a problem. The nets weren't going to be much use. But we took them with us all the same. When we reached the house there was already a crowd gathered – a small one, but growing by the minute, mainly children on holiday from school for August. Every face, including ours, was turned upwards to the roof of the house where a confident figure could be seen grasping a chimney pot and every so often making gestures reminiscent of Churchill at a Victory Parade. From time to time an apple or hunk of bread was shied upwards. Most came down again quicker than they'd gone up, but some found the roof, and Freda was very appreciative. Our hopes of an early capture dwindled to zero. The crowd continued to grow, and very shortly the Press were on the scene, making the most of the story and giving us helpful hints.

'You could put a ladder up. We could hand you the nets.'

I explained that this wasn't a good idea. I had no wish to end up in Hillingdon Hospital.

'Come on,' I said to Jenny at last, 'we might as well leave her for now. She'll not come down while there's this crowd.' We decided to have a look later.

Much later we did have a look. There was still a crowd under the street lights. Freda looked well set for the night.

Early next morning we were back again. But not early enough. Already the children were out. Freda had

obviously spent a nice balmy summer night by the
chimney pots, and was by now enjoying her breakfast
that came obligingly through the air. We tried again later
in the day. Then early the following day. And so on. But
far from showing signs of abandoning her perch, every
day seemed to consolidate it. By now a television crew
had arrived and begun filming. They not only ensured
that Freda would be a celebrity, but attracted even greater
crowds, and these would multiply even further once
their work had gone out on the air.

The television début of Freda, in fact, effectively put an
end to whatever slim hope we had of capturing her. From
that moment the place was under siege. People arrived in
cars and made an evening of it. They came by bus, and
they came by tube. Hot dog men seized their opportunity, and Freda's diet was enriched with mustard and
sausage.

By now she was known as Fearless Freda, Queen of the
Rooftops. She certainly had no reason to fear capture.
Not even the weather helped. It was continuously hot,
and no sign of a storm that might possibly have driven
her down. The owners of the houses had a difficult time,
quite apart from the noise, commotion and litter on their
doorsteps. They had to sit out this rare English heatwave
with every door and window firmly locked and barred
against Freda. We knew she would be into any house left
open, because one morning I had a telephone call from a
very cross woman. She suggested the R.S.P.C.A. should
do more to try and catch Freda.

'Do you know,' she said, 'I'd made rhubarb and
custard for our Sunday lunch and forgot to close the
window. When I went into the kitchen to get it, it had
gone!'

I said I was sorry. But there was nothing we could do.

Two months went by. Still the weather held. Still the
crowds turned out. Still we couldn't catch Freda.

There was talk of baited traps. There was also, rather
more sinister, talk of police marksmen. Luckily, the
latter was a non-starter. Humane considerations aside,
the police would never have been able to shoot her at

night, the only time when there were no crowds. And to shoot her during the day would have meant great hostility from the spectators – and not much good for the police image.

It was left to Jenny to supply the crucial brainwave. Amidst all the other work at the Hostel, Freda was very much on our minds, even though she seemed to have become an almost permanent part of our lives.

She came to me one morning. 'The thing she goes for is open windows,' she said.

'Yes,' I said, not quite seeing where this was leading.

'Well,' argued Jenny, 'if we can get into one of the houses and leave a window open we *might* be able to get her.'

'Well, it may be worth a try,' I said, not very convinced. Once again we collected the catching nets, and went across the road. We talked to one of the householders, explained the plan above the murmur of the crowd encouraging Freda to do her stuff above us, and went inside. Jenny, meanwhile, had equipped herself with half a pound of tempting-looking grapes.

We went up to the small bedroom at the front of the house. To the window catch we attached a length of cord we had brought with us. We placed one or two of the grapes invitingly on the window-sill, and the rest on the floor. We then led the cord out of the door, having opened the window wide. The bedroom door was then closed with the cord coming out under it. 'Right,' Jenny said, 'I'll go outside and watch. You stay here and I'll let you know.'

Time ticked on after she went, and I sat on the stairs wondering whether anything like it had ever happened before in R.S.P.C.A. history. Then I heard a shout from Jenny. 'She's in.' In her perambulations around the roof Freda had spied the open window and been powerless to resist the temptation. She was in the bedroom. I pulled the cord as hard as I could and heard the window slam shut.

Fearless Freda's reign on the rooftops was over. When we opened the bedroom door there she was sitting on the floor making short work of the grapes, and within a minute we had her, very gently, in the nets.

So ended the strangest interlude ever at the Hostel. But it was not without an illuminating tailpiece. Shortly after she was captured, the airline announced that it would meet claims for any damage caused by Freda during her two months on the loose. The letters began to pour in. 'Dear Sir, Regarding your announcement, I wish to claim for a broken TV aerial and one damaged chimney pot plus several missing tiles...' The postmarks ranged from Hillingdon to as far as Staines, and even Windsor. Yet during her entire spell of freedom, Freda had never left the houses opposite the Hostel on the A4. Which seems to prove that where cunning is concerned, monkeys have nothing on humans.

9

In the News

Fearless Freda provided the longest-running drama we'd had so far, and certainly showed us how the unexpected was constantly to be our lot. Equally unexpected was the incident of the tortoises. Many thousands of tortoises arrive in Britain every year for the pet trade. The trouble is that, out of the enormous number of tortoises that arrive here for sale, only a small proportion survive, probably no more than one in ten. The reason is the English weather. If the temperature's not correct they won't eat, and if they don't eat they can't store enough food to carry them through hibernation. So what price a tortoise's prospects when we get Test Matches and Wimbledon washed out in June and July, and hailstorms in August?

The R.S.P.C.A., needless to say, disapprove of the tortoise trade. Having said that, I must confess that I myself keep a pet tortoise called Ossie, of whom Peg and I are very fond; but he came to us more than twelve years ago in rather unusual circumstances. His original owner was taken into a geriatric ward in Hounslow Hospital, and the R.S.P.C.A. were called in to deal with the animals she'd left behind. These included two billy goats, whose presence was well advertised before we had the front door open more than a couple of inches. If we'd had a kind of geiger counter for smells, it would have gone off the clock.

There was also the tortoise, which I decided I would find a home for; because I could find no one willing to take him, the home we found was our own. Ossie has been with us ever since; he goes into hibernation in October in a box in the outside W.C., and wakes up almost unfailingly to the day on Peg's birthday, 16 March, after which he doesn't get round to eating again for a fortnight or three weeks. An interval of nearly six months between meals seems a bit extravagant to me, but tortoises seem to take everything in life at their own slow pace.

Even with expert attention, tortoises are not easy pets to keep, but at least these days they travel here in better conditions than they used to on their journeys from Casablanca, Morocco, Turkey, and, at one time, Russia even. There are now laws to enforce humane packing. These ensure that the tortoises must be housed in boxes, shallow enough to prevent them climbing over one another, and not, as used to be all too common, cruelly heaped anyhow in containers one on top of another so that many did not survive the flight. But there were no laws in force on the day that 6,000 tortoises arrived on our doorstep without any previous warning.

We unloaded more than a hundred big Ali Baba-type baskets into the Hostel, all nearly three feet tall by two-foot-six wide. The Hostel shortly began to look like a scene from *The Arabian Nights*. That is, until we began to open up the baskets. Inside, piled up regardless of sex or size, each contained more than fifty tortoises. The baskets had simply been filled, the tops put on, then wired down. It was unbelievable. Had it happened today, the shipper would certainly have been fined under the International Air Transport Association law, and the all-powerful Transit of Animals General Order (1973).

The only reason we had this unlucky cargo wished on us was that the documentation was not in order, and we had to look after it until the right forms were completed and signed. Thus, we had our first eye-opening view of what went on in the tortoise trade. Had the documentation been correct the tortoises would simply have gone straight from the aircraft to the importer, and we would have been none the wiser.

As it was, we had tortoises everywhere. Jenny Stansfield was by now the senior girl, and in addition we had taken on other staff, mainly to cope with the monkey traffic. It was as well we had. With every one of us working at it, it took us hours to unpack the baskets and ferry each tortoise individually into the paddock, which in the end was an incredible horizon to horizon panorama of nothing but tortoises.

With 6,000 tortoises came feeding problems on a corresponding scale. The local greengrocers made a bomb out of it all. We kept up a shuttle service between the Hostel and the vegetable shops, buying sack upon sack of cabbages and cauliflowers, box after box of tomatoes, and loads of root vegetables to keep them all happy. This went on for several days while the documentation was being sorted out. Looking out of my office window I sometimes had the strange feeling that I was marooned on an island set in a moving sea of dark

mottled shells. At other times I imagined I was in a film called *Planet of the Tortoises*, in which I played the part of the only human being left on earth.

When the importer was finally ready to take delivery, he rang up and he said his name was Gosley and he was coming down personally. I told him he would have to provide proper boxes.

'Proper boxes? I don't get you. What's wrong with the baskets they came in?'

I explained the R.S.P.C.A. point of view as best I could, then, with no justification whatsoever, added that he would be liable to prosecution if he didn't come up with some better way of transporting the tortoises.

In the end Mr Gosley said he'd see what he could do, telling me along the way how much money he'd already lost with the delay, that any more delay in finding proper containers would cost him still more, that most of the consignment was already sold in advance to pet shops, that it could be ruination for him, etc., etc. I told him we were doing him a favour, and hung up. But when he arrived the following day at least he'd seen reason. Perhaps the bogus prosecution threat had worked.

He was small, hunched-up into an old raincoat, and looked a bit like a tortoise himself. Not at all the Gosley I'd imagined from the big talk on the phone. But he'd come in a van which, for size, would have done credit to Pickfords. In it were stacked up an immense load of long cartons and boxes. For this at least he got some credit. He'd been down to Covent Garden early that morning (in those days still a fruit, vegetable and flower market) and collected scores of boxes that had been used for packing long-stemmed flowers such as gladioli. They were ideal, no more than five inches high, about two foot six inches long, and two foot wide. Some were cardboard; some, even better, were made of wood, with hinged lids.

'Now then,' said Gosley, after doing his bit carting the boxes into our front reception area, 'where are they?'

'I'll show you,' I said, and led him to the paddock.

'Blimey,' he said, stopping in his tracks, struck almost

speechless by the sight of what, after all, was a paddock full of profit for him.

'How long's it going to take to pack them?' he asked, finally.

'Quite a time. You can wait in my office if you like, and help yourself to coffee. There's a machine in the corridor.'

He thought for a moment, and must have realized he was in for a long wait. 'No,' he said, 'I'll go and have a kip in the van.'

Which he did, leaving the girls and me to set to once again, this time grading and sorting and packing the tortoises according to size. We couldn't put in, say, half a dozen big ones, and two tiddlers to fill up the box. We had to do it more methodically and humanely than that, so it was all a bit like making endless live Cotswold stone walls. It took most of the day, but finally Gosley was able to drive his cargo away, and we all thankfully knocked off. That night we didn't need to count tortoises to get to sleep.

But it wasn't quite the end of the tortoise story. The postscript came two or three months later. We began to notice a change coming over the foliage in the paddock. The tortoise invasion had taken place in early summer. Now it was getting on for autumn. We saw strange, unfamiliar vegetable shapes where none had been before, and a profusion of green plants: tomatoes, peas, beans, even an odd cabbage or two. The tortoises, through entirely natural processes, had bequeathed us an entire vegetable garden!

This bonus apart, the Hostel owes a great deal to tortoises, or, more accurately, to one tortoise called Annabel. If it hadn't been for Annabel, and, shortly before her arrival, a tragic event at Heathrow, the Hostel might never have had its name and work put before the public as it did – give or take Fearless Freda, who hadn't exactly provided the kind of publicity we needed.

First the tragic event, with the irony that out of it should have come some good. This is going back to the fifties when the R.A.F. was operating its V-Force of bombers, so-called because the names of all the aircraft, all big jets, began with the letter V: Valiant, Victor, and Vulcan. The Vulcan survives today and came into the news most recently for its long trip to the Falkland Islands.

But this was long before the Falklands crisis. A Vulcan, piloted by Air Marshal Sir Harry Broadhurst, then chief of Bomber Command, had been on a tour of Australia and New Zealand. On the way back it was due to land at Heathrow. The runway in use was only a few hundred yards from the Hostel (by this time the Heathrow runways had been extended and it was at last possible to see that we were actually part of an airport).

I happened to be looking out when the Vulcan was on its approach. It seemed to be coming in normally, the jets throttled back, the whine and roar growing louder, until, all at once, I saw it change its attitude. The nose canted up, and at the same time the Vulcan, like a gigantic white paper dart, began to climb away very steeply. The pilot hadn't got the approach right and had decided to do an overshoot.

What happened next was horrific, and took almost less time than it takes to write this. The Vulcan appeared to stop climbing, and to hang suspended in the air for a split-second. Then it toppled and simply fell out of the sky. Two objects, black dots against the blue, were flung clear and came down on parachutes. But even before the parachutes opened, the Vulcan had hit the runway and there was an enormous sheet of flame and a great billowing cloud of black smoke.

I learned later that Sir Harry and the co-pilot had managed to use their ejector seats to escape: but – such was the design of the V-Bombers – there was no escape for the other three crew members who sat on a 'backbench' behind the pilot and facing aft. All three perished in the crash.

Later that morning, I went into the Peggy Bedford pub, close to the airport. The Vulcan tragedy had brought the Press and television down, and the camera crews were having a break as I went in. Everyone seemed to be discussing the crash, and I was no exception. I said to the then landlady, Miss Shoebrook, how terrible it had been, and that I'd seen it all happen. The next thing I knew was that one of the television people was at my side, asking me to go up to Lime Grove and be interviewed as an 'eye-witness'. And that, in its sad and paradoxical way, is what started the Hostel on the road to publicity from the B.B.C., both sound and television, and countless newspapers and magazines.

But what set the seal on all this, now that the media were aware of our existence, was a call not long afterwards from Passenger Arrivals to say that there was a tortoise walking through Emigration and along the passageway! Could we do something about it? From the grim tone of the voice at the other end of the telephone it sounded as if they had a brontosaurus loose in the Terminal, not just a tortoise. I took our ambulance and went off at full speed.

I reached Passport Control. 'Where is it?' I asked. They all knew what 'it' was.

'Down the other end,' I was told. Going down to one end of the hall I found what I was looking for, and the emigration man with the doom-laden voice who had spoken on the phone. The tortoise was in a cardboard box on his desk.

'What happened?' I asked.

He wasn't very forthcoming, and I thought that if Old Crusty in Customs had a brother, this must be him.

'Don't really know,' he said. 'Somebody must have been taking a tortoise abroad with them – don't ask me why – and it must have got out of the hand luggage. First thing I knew I spotted it going up that corridor there, walking along near the wall...'

He made it sound like a Panzer division on the march. I decided there was no point in hanging around. Since it was near lunchtime I took myself plus tortoise off to the bar. Sitting at the bar with a half pint I looked at the escapee, and saw it was female. You can tell by the shape of the underside of the shell: the male is concave, and the female flat.

At that moment Chris Bramwell, who was on the *Daily Telegraph*, came up. 'What've you got there, Neville?' he asked.

I took the tortoise out of her box, let her have a tentative foray round the olives and peanuts, put her back, and told him the story, or as much of it as I knew.

'What's its name?' he asked.

What a strange question, I thought.

'Name? I've no idea. It didn't have a passport, you know.'

'But it ought to *have* a name.'

I bought him a drink to head him off the subject. It didn't work.

'What about Annabel?' said Chris, after some thought.

'Why not?' I said, 'Cheers.' I was beginning to wish that the Emigration people had found some other way of dealing with the problem rather than involving me. Except, of course, I would then have wanted to know why the R.S.P.C.A. hadn't been told.

I took Annabel, as she now was, back to the Hostel in the ambulance. I decided we would have to keep her for a time to see if there was a claim for her. Then the phone rang. It was the B.B.C. on the line. Would I go down to the television studios with Annabel, and be interviewed by Cliff Michelmore for the *Tonight* programme?

I agreed, and put the phone down, before they could change their minds. How about that, I thought. Chris Bramwell must have been doing his stuff with his contacts. What a good thing he'd thought of a name for her! *Tonight* was a very popular early evening magazine programme which exploited the news in a fresh and unusual way. I was thrilled, though a bit nervous, at the idea of appearing on it.

So down to Lime Grove I went with Annabel, now in a classier container than her old cardboard box. Cliff Michelmore did his usual expert and good-natured interview. Afterwards he told me that he'd remembered seeing me interviewed after the Vulcan crash and talking a bit about the Hostel: 'So, at least, I could ask you some intelligent questions!'

Michelmore's intelligent questions brought another response the following day: the phone at the Hostel hardly stopped ringing. We took down endless offers of a good home for the little tortoise. In the end she was not claimed by her owner, and we did find a good home for her – at the London Zoo, which we thought was best despite the calls of so many good-hearted people. So Annabel passed from our sight. But she really started something. From the time of her strange walk through Emigration and into our lives, the Hostel was never out of the news.

Admittedly the hundreds of headlines we got over the years mostly played up the grimmer side of our activities. They ran (all genuine examples) on the line of AGONY BY AIR FREIGHT, FIGHT TO SAVE 590 MONKEYS, and CAR-GOES OF HORROR AT HEATHROW. But without the Press and the forceful way they described what was going on, we would never have made the headway we did in building up public pressure in the fight to beat the conditions.

One story that never made the headlines, and might have made a big splash if it had, concerned the inaugural flight of the V.C.10 airliner. This aircraft, designed in the fifties, was yet another piece of engineering that ought, like the Comet, to have ensured the future for the British aircraft industry. But, in the end, even our own national airlines sold us out to the Americans.

Yet hopes were high on the day the V.C.10 first flew into Heathrow from Australia and New Zealand. After a record-breaking run, the tarmac was crowded with V.I.P.s waiting to welcome it. I was one of the crowd, but not as a V.I.P. Among all the exchange of chat and pleasantries I was one of the few who knew there might be an anxious moment or so on arrival. In my pocket I had a signal from the aircraft to B.O.A.C. It read: Emergency. Squirrels broken loose in hold. Suspected entry main battery compartment. Contact R.S.P.C.A. and advise.'

I'd been handed the signal only half an hour or so before the V.C.10 was due to arrive. My first thought was that it was a hoax. I couldn't see how there could be squirrels aboard an aircraft from Australia. Then it dawned. The aircraft must have stopped on the way in India and taken on board a cargo of tree rats: these were a frequent cargo from India, quite engaging creatures who run up and down the trees out there. Although striped, they do resemble squirrels. They were harmless enough, but very inquisitive. I stood in the crowd sweating gently at the thought of what might happen if they became too inquisitive about the aircraft's batteries, and hence its main electricity supply...

By now, all eyes were focusing eastwards, and the buzz of conversation had become more animated as an aircraft approached that did not look like a normal aircraft, because there were no engines either in the wing roots or under the wings: they were up at the tail. It was the V.C.10. Unlike the rest of the crowd, I found it hard to concentrate, despite some relief that it was actually there, whining in apparently normally on the approach, and sinking towards the runway. In *my* mind's eye there was a tree rat poised over a vital circuit, about to investigate as it might a new species of nut-tree ... I stared at the V.C.10, willing it down safely. It looked steady on the final approach...then a brief screech of tyres, a fleeting puff or two of rubber wafting back and disappearing in the slipstream, and the thunder of reverse thrust as the aircraft decelerated down the runway. I breathed deeply, and pulled the signal from my pocket. It was little more than a screw of paper that, unconsciously, I'd been holding onto on the approach.

Eventually the very first V.C.10 to appear at Heathrow taxied round to the hard-standing in front of the crowd. I was there waiting as the steps were wheeled out. As soon as the first door was open I showed the signal, crumpled as it was, to the B.O.A.C. man in charge, and I was first up the ladder to the flight-deck.

The captain was still in his seat, shirt-sleeved, and still directing various post-flight checks. 'R.S.P.C.A.,' I said loudly.

The effect, suitable in the circumstances, perhaps, was

electric. 'Right,' he said, immediately getting out of his seat. He led the way along the cramped flight-deck, and came to a panel in the flooring.

'They're under there,' he said, tapping the panel with his foot, and, over his shoulder, 'Can someone bring a Philips screwdriver, please...?'

I learned that the tree rats had broken out of their boxes in the mail and baggage hold, and somehow got along a conduit into this main battery compartment under our feet. Until I could deal with them, the freight doors had to be kept locked.

'How many are there?' I asked.

'At least two, but possibly more,' said the captain. 'We only found them because of a circuit fault and a chance inspection down there.'

He handed me a torch and I lowered myself through the narrow panel opening and down a ladder, aware that until I found the tree rats the main doors could not be opened. I flashed the light around the compartment: it was like something out of *Dr Who*, with rows of black batteries, wires and terminals leading everywhere – and, for me, the thought that an Alien Force was lurking. At first, however, the Alien Force kept well hidden. I gingerly eased my way around, then, suddenly, caught a suspicion of movement out of the corner of my eye. I shone the torch down behind one of the banks of batteries. There they were, a pair of tree rats, eyes glinting like brilliants in the light, and, astonishingly, seemingly content to huddle there. I moved forward as unobtrusively as I could, putting the torch on a battery top to give me both hands free. Then a swift, hopeful, grab, and they were mine.

'Got you,' I said, making my way back to the panel opening. By this time one of my staff had followed me with a basket and was on the flight-deck waiting. 'Here's the first two,' I said, reaching up and handing them over.

Luckily they proved also to be the last. I went over the battery room twice more, but there were no other invaders, nor in the conduit, nor in the hold, which I also inspected.

'All clear,' I reported, back on the flight–deck.

'Well done,' said the captain, and grinned, '...quite a relief.'

From the cabin window I saw the crowd of V.I.P.s and B.O.A.C. officials waiting, unaware, and impatient at the delay. The captain put on his uniform jacket and cap.

'Come on,' he said, leading the way to the steps, 'you can come and listen to my speech. I shan't tell them we nearly didn't make it!'

10

Airborne

Despite the welcome new publicity, we ourselves didn't seem to be doing enough to tackle the monkey business where it really mattered: in India and Africa. However well the monkeys were crated they would still suffer from the very fact of flying. Not until the monkey trade ceased altogether would this be prevented. Bad crating was a different matter. Despite all the representations by the R.S.P.C.A. and by the airlines themselves, the problem continued. Then, at last, there came an opportunity.

A consignment of baboons arrived from Africa. It was among the worst cases we ever had at the Hostel: an enormous proportion were dead on arrival. They had died in flight not merely through stress and strain, but mostly through suffocation. This had been caused, first, by the familiar, deadly practice of putting animals in containers far too small for them. The baboons had been crammed into boxes designed for vervets of half the size. They were bent double, hunched up – and mostly dead. The other cause was that the shipper had put mosquito netting over the air grilles. The fine mesh had not only stopped any stray mosquito getting in, but air as well. It was a terrible sight as crate after crate was opened, and each one revealed the same awful mortality to us. The Press were alerted, and the papers the following day carried big stories. But, more important, British United Airways (B.U.A.) were so appalled at the scale of the deaths among the baboons that they decided that some direct action was imperative. At their own expense they offered to fly me out to Africa, with a senior R.S.P.C.A. superintendent, to investigate the cruelty side. My role would be to discuss practical ways of avoiding this sort of animal disaster. It was the breakthrough I had long been waiting for.

The following Saturday we boarded a B.U.A. Britannia, the big turbo-prop airliner that was so quiet it was nicknamed 'The Whispering Giant', and took off for Nairobi. A stop in Entebbe gave us just enough time to have breakfast and discuss problems with the local R.S.P.C.A. officials. Nairobi we reached fourteen hours after leaving Heathrow. I was booked into the Stanley Hotel, famous as a safari centre, and I couldn't help thinking that the big game I would be after were all human beings: the monkey shippers.

There followed days of discussions. The shippers themselves were all too willing to meet us. After all, it was in their interest to improve packaging, because the less the mortality, the greater the chance of repeating orders. £.s.d. again. Having made that comment, I don't suggest that the shippers wished intentionally to be cruel. I merely say that money was the prime consideration, as with all businessmen. It was an activity of which the R.S.P.C.A. greatly disapproved. Yet, because the monkey trade was quite legal we had to recognize its existence. Moreover, we had to do what we could to alleviate the suffering of the creatures involved.

The shippers I met first were fairly high-powered and mostly had reasonable packaging standards anyway. It was good to meet them on their home ground, which happened to be the holding station for monkeys at an airfield (not the main international one) in the bush outside Nairobi. I then met the men who ran the smaller-scale businesses. Their packaging standards left a lot to be desired, mostly because of ignorance. Once again, we had very useful talks, and I passed on all the ideas I could, including suggestions from the bigger shippers as to how things could be improved. I stood by, after a week, for my return to Heathrow feeling I had at last struck a blow on behalf of the monkeys.

The aircraft was a D.C.7, the regular Saturday night animal freighter out of Nairobi. Just as I'd learned a lot during the week from the monkey shippers, so the flight home was also to be an eye-opener. I had met this very same freighter and others like it on arrival at London Airport and knew – or rather could imagine – what a flight aboard it was like. But imagination proved no substitute for the reality.

When I arrived at Nairobi Airport, the loading of the livestock was already well under way. At least this was a very impressive and efficient operation. Ninety boxes of monkeys, ten to a box, were being stacked along the fuselage. Then there were crates of finches, crates marked 'Highly Poisonous' containing reptiles, and the usual quota of domestic dogs and cats. Last, but certainly not least, was a baby elephant. As I stood there watching under the African stars I really did feel like a modern Noah witnessing embarkation on an up-to-date ark. Also, with the odd smell of slightly rotting vegetation in my nostrils, the characteristic scent of the tropics, it came home to me for the first time how totally unnatural the experience was for the animals.

At last, having watched most of the animal cargo aboard, I made for the aircraft.

Take-off time came soon enough. With a bloom of mauve flame at each engine exhaust the D.C.7 gathered speed and lifted off; very soon the flarepath was just a small, ever-diminishing V of orange light behind and below. A handful of men, plus 1,000 monkeys, birds and reptiles, were aloft in the African night bound for England. It was a strange thought.

After things had settled down I went up on the flight-deck and made my number with the captain and crew. It was a different world up there, with orange lighting and glowing instruments, a contrast to the long vista of boxes, of bright peering eyes, of mynah birds silenced only by the engine noise, and the baby elephant looking trustingly and innocently out of her crate.

'Make yourself at home, Mr Whittaker,' said the

captain, 'Come up here any time you're not with the animals – I'll be doing regular checks myself as well. Pull down that seat there near Harry, he won't mind.' In the dim cabin lighting I saw Harry grin. He was the engineer, and he obligingly pulled down the rumble-seat for me. The captain continued to be thoughtful and kind throughout the flight, and not only to me. He was very much at pains to see that the animals and birds in his charge got on as well as they could. After what I'd seen at the Hostel, it was reassuring to know that there was this amount of care aboard a freighter.

'I can always get you a Scotch,' he said with a big grin.

'Now you're talking.'

The flight wore on. We stopped for fuel, water and stores, and the captain made a point of asking whether there was anything required for the animals. I took turn and turn about with the others, alternately cat-napping either in the hold or up on the flight-deck, and helping with the animals. We doled out the food for the monkeys – sweet potatoes and pineapples – and replenished the water for them and the birds. There was also the task, which I saw for the first time for myself, of removing the monkeys and birds that did not survive. It was a doleful business. Here were we, quite able to fly at 20,000 feet in a pressurized tube of metal with wings, but it was too much for some of the monkeys and finches.

In addition to these tasks there was also the little baby elephant. She, despite her size, kept us well occupied – and we didn't mind one bit. She really was tiny, and I knew that she had shamefully been taken from her mother and shipped out when she should still have been feeding on natural milk. We spent a lot of time sitting by her little box and keeping her happy; we shared a contempt for the purposes of her totally unnecessary journey. She was destined for a cabaret in Brussels. I wondered what kind of sub-human impresario could possibly have thought up such a cruel gimmick to draw the crowds. Feeding her took quite a lot of patience. The shippers at least had taken the trouble to provide condensed milk. This we mixed with water, and fed her from a bottle by tube, lifting her tiny trunk so that she could suck the milk in – or some of it anyway. We usually had more milk on our clothes by the end of feeding time than she, bless her, had managed to swallow.

At last we were circling the Dunsfold radio beacon on the final stage of the flight to Heathrow. There was unbroken cloud below, so we were back over England, and shortly afterwards we were on the approach to London Airport. Nairobi seemed a world away, yet all round us were the reminders that we had actually been there. And not only the sight of boxes of animals reminded us. By now, after the heat of the cabin, our very clothes and hair were impregnated by animal smells. B.O. took on a new dimension. So did enforced insomnia – I hadn't managed any proper sleep. I knew by now that life on board the freighters not only took a toll of the animals, but exacted some sort of due from the human beings who looked after them too. We were exhausted. But, as the wheels touched the Heathrow runway, I was profoundly grateful for the entire experience. Seeing was believing.

When I arrived back the Hostel looked exactly as it had done only ten days before, almost maddeningly familiar. All the same, with all that had happened to me in such a brief time, it seemed somehow out of focus. I knew my perspective on my work and that of the entire Hostel had been quite altered.

Eventually I got home. Peg was appalled at how tired I looked; twenty-four hours' rest was ordered, and very readily taken. I spent most of it sleeping, but during the time I was awake I couldn't help thinking of the baby elephant we'd spent so much time with. I imagined her sitting happily in her box on her journey to Brussels.

Unfortunately this was only a thought. A few days later word came through to the Hostel that the little baby elephant had died in the aircraft taking her towards her unchosen, tawdry future. I felt very sad and, not for the first or last time in similar circumstances, very angry.

On the trip to Nairobi I think I achieved something as far as African shippers were concerned. But India was a different matter. With all shippers the greatest problem of all was that there were no regulations, nothing laid down by law, no minimum standards that could be enforced. Even more incredible was the fact that there did not exist one single authoritative piece of advice on the subject of crating livestock for air travel, whether monkeys or Indian finches, tropical fish or alligators, elephants or tigers, dogs or cats. We were aware of this lack, and had set up meetings to discuss how we could overcome it, and collect such advice together into what I might call an Animals' Charter.

There were gleams of hope, however, and shortly I undertook another trip abroad. I had the idea of an Animals' Charter specifically in mind, as well as wanting to have a close look at conditions in India and the Far East. Singapore was my next port of call, flown there in luxury in a Comet 4.

I found it a beguiling place, from the bicycle rickshaws to the palm trees it seemed a tropical yet not a tropical place. So unlike Africa, much more subtle, though many of the stage props and scenery were the same. Perhaps it was the people: I took to them at once because they never appeared to resent anyone being white. Perhaps it was an illusion, but they had their own ways of being equal and independent. Against this there was an air of faded Empire in the breeze, summed up in the Raffles Hotel, still there, yet not quite there as it used to be.

I was, in fact, booked into the Raffles Hotel, and was amazed on being shown to my room to find they had provided not merely writing paper, but writing paper with my name in gold lettering on it. NEVILLE WHITTAKER in gold lettering served to illustrate a fine irony – the contrast between the bright lights and superficial luxury of Singapore and what I knew to be the shady side of the island's activities. Here was I, an R.S.P.C.A. representative, in the very centre of what was beginning to be one of the world's biggest cross-roads for illegal trafficking in wild animals, birds, and reptiles. Singapore, by an accident of geography, is situated right in the middle of jungle areas where wild life abounds: South-east Asia, Indonesia, Borneo. Not only that, but it is a relatively short air journey from Australia, with its own different forms of wild life – though here there were already export bans.

The trade was in its infancy when I was there. It was to multiply a hundredfold in only a few years, and dealers in Singapore and elsewhere (notably Bangkok) were to make fortunes out of animal smuggling. They ran operations that for sheer sophistication and intrigue behind the law were straight out of a James Bond thriller. It had a terrible effect on wild life populations. But the more progressive countries desperately legislated to stop the export of their increasingly endangered species, the more the illicit dealers flourished, finding cleverer ways to beat the regulations. And they were aided by the biggest loopholes of all: in the West, where the demand came from, for many years there were insufficient import controls to match the export bans in the East.

The West, of course, provided the biggest impelling

force of all: money. Not just ordinary money, but millions of pounds and dollars. At the heart of it all were the pathetic cravings of money-no-object millionaire collectors to whom living creatures might just as well have been paintings or postage stamps – and as with those collectors' items, the rarer (i.e. more endangered) the animal, the more desired it became, and the more crazy money would be paid for it.

What hope was there of stopping the traffic when such attitudes existed? When one man could earn as much as £7,000 in a single trip from Sydney to Zurich with a single consignment of rare snakes, or £4,500 for smuggling a single pair of golden-shouldered rosellas (a kind of parakeet) from Queensland to London? When in Australia syndicates had begun to operate with their own ships, aircraft and four-wheel-drive vehicles, catching and crating anything they could lay their hands on – birds, lizards, goannas – and were turning over millions of pounds?

I, meanwhile, was in Singapore to look into the more legitimate, though also lucrative, brokerage in living creatures. This included tropical fish, which had become (once again mainly because of fad and fashion in the West) very big business indeed. One of the first things I did from my room in the Raffles Hotel was to telephone someone to whom I had an introduction: the owner of the biggest tropical fish export firm, which traded under the name of Tay Way Yong.

His real name was Harris (despite the fact that he was Chinese), and he kindly spent a great deal of time with me, told me much I had not known about tropical fish, and took me down to the big covered market in Singapore which, in among the fruit and veg stalls, had a section dealing exclusively in tropical fish. On one side it was filled with rows and rows of metal tanks, all containing every conceivable kind of tropical fish, from the neon tetras that had become so popular in the Western World to the fierce fighting fish. They had all been caught in the streams and rivers of the forests, and were kept alive now with oxygen bubbling through their tanks. The sheer scale of the operation was astonishing. By the side of the tanks sat small Chinese boys all busy catching the fish and putting them into plastic bags for export, with water which was sometimes coloured blue or green with antibiotic. In the corner of the market I noticed something that looked like a strange red pyramid, a mini-mountain almost. On closer inspection it turned out to be the supply of worms – also caught in the forest rivers – for the fish.

I watched, fascinated, the whole teeming activity of the market, particularly as the boys, when they had filled so many plastic bags, took them to a separate section where they put them in polystyrene boxes for shipment abroad – some of them destined for our Hostel, the idea of which seemed at that moment very remote indeed.

A great deal of good came from meeting the head of Tay Way Yong. We got on very well indeed, and as a token, when I visited his bungalow, he offered me a handsom orang-utan to take home as a present. Sadly, it was of course impossible for me to accept this, and all the more difficult to resist because she climbed up and tried to give me a kiss as we sat on the verandah! But instead I was given a fine musical box which Peg treasures to this day.

Tropical fish formed one big side of the Singapore animal export trade. The other concerned birds, mostly members of the parrot family such as the sulphur crested cockatoo, as well as many birds smuggled out of Australia, and Java sparrows, which came out of Singapore in their thousands. Once again I was able to have a lot of useful discussion on the packaging problems, particularly regarding the Java sparrow, where we were able to solve a problem that had lasted as long as that particular bird had been coming into the Hostel.

The perches for the Java sparrows had always been mounted one above the other. Birds, being subject like everyone else to natural processes, only possibly more frequently, this resulted in the Java sparrows on the lower perches turning up in the U.K. not looking their best, to say the least. As I went round I managed to get over a fresh idea to the dealers.

'Why not make the perches like seats in a football stadium, in tiers?' I suggested. The dealers, unaware that their original perches caused any problems at all, agreed to try my idea, and in time we got it working. Another small step forward.

By the time I left Singapore, in fact, I felt we had achieved a great deal, and that there was common ground appearing for what I most wanted: a comprehensive document covering all aspects of transport of animals by air. Appropriately, perhaps, I was not due to travel back in luxury. Instead I was to join the weekly animal freighter on the first stages of its journey as far as Delhi.

I was down at the airport in good time, and there was the familiar aircraft. But instead of the very orderly loading process that I had seen in Nairobi, the tarmac here was bustling with people, livestock shippers personally bringing their loads to the aircraft, a great deal of haggling going on for some reason, and, mixed up with all of this, the owners of dogs and cats who, standing by with their pets in little boxes, looked lost in the confusion. It was all a great contrast not only to the scene at Nairobi, but to procedures of the present day when animals have to be at the freight shed six hours before a flight, and no one, for security reasons, is allowed anywhere near an aircraft. But that's progress!

Looking back I preferred the informality of airports in those days, not only in Singapore but back at Heathrow, where changes over the years brought stricter and stricter controls so that in the end one almost had to have a permit to breathe. However, this was 1960. As a result I was able to wander about freely on the tarmac, seeing exactly what happened to the livestock. I was even able to comfort one lady dog-owner who was distraught at the idea of her pet flying, and in her mind almost certainly dying. An airline official brought her along and introduced me as the R.S.P.C.A. official who would be travelling with the animals. The relief on her face was totally unjustified, but a joy to see.

When I finally went on board there was the usual mixed cargo already stacked. It included some tiny leopard–cat kittens from Thailand, who looked very dehydrated and distressed even at the start of the flight. They were barely off their mother's milk, and would need feeding regularly throughout the journey.

Leopard–cat kittens and baby stump-tailed and pig-tailed monkeys had been through the Hostel, so we knew about the traffic in these very young animals. But here I was seeing the despatch end of things, and this made me determined that, when I got back home, I would make representations to the Thai Embassy about it. (In time the Thai Embassy, because of the pressure on it, persuaded its government to ban the export of such young animals, so I was glad to have had a hand in helping to stop the traffic.)

Next to the leopard–cat kittens was a big consignment of Java sparrows, several thousand birds. All were on the original type of perch, and those on the lowest rung were already bearing evidence to that effect. Sellotaped to the side of one of the crates was a letter addressed to 'Dr (*sic*) Whittaker. R.S.P.C.A.' It said: 'Hope you have a good trip back to England. If you ever get any orders for Java sparrows, don't forget to send them on to me.' It was signed by the dealer I thought was keenest on my stadium idea. Oh well!

So we took off. The flight, as far as routine went, was a repeat of the previous one, except that this time I watched out carefully as we got airborne to see what, if any, were the reactions of the livestock to the first sensation of flying. There was one, however; the only unusual thing I noted was that the cabin lighting, dim as it was, seemed to prevent the birds from going to sleep. And on this flight there was no poor little baby elephant to look after and chat to. Instead the leopard–cat kittens needed particular attention.

This, and being able from time to time to take the dogs one by one from their boxes and walk them down the aircraft towards the rear where there was no livestock (it was noisier perhaps, but in its way as private as a park on a Sunday morning), kept me fully occupied until we were on the approach to New Delhi Airport.

I'd immediately taken to Singapore, and just as quickly didn't take to Delhi. There was an oppressive sense that the British Raj had gone, but that India hadn't yet managed to replace it. There were grand buildings, though they looked in need of paint and repair, and on the other hand, beggars and squalor. Big hotels with apparently every facility for businessmen, but prohibition in the bars. And in contrast to the luxuriance of Singapore, dust, heat and dirt.

My first call was a visit to the local R.S.P.C.A. We ran an animal sanctuary in the old part of the city. It was a red stone building with an outer perimeter and a straw-roofed structure divided into sections for dogs, cattle, cats, and other creatures that were brought in for treatment. A far cry, I thought, from Sister Mabel's in Camberwell. The principle may have been the same, but, as I soon learned from the vets and R.S.P.C.A. personnel I chatted to, it was not easy to persuade the citizens of Delhi to bring animals in. I found it in the end rather a sad place because, with famine and starvation rife, and religious attitudes to animals complicating matters, animal life was not regarded in the same light as in England. I felt there was little I could do to help, and was quite glad when the time came for me to meet two of the biggest monkey shippers, whose offices were also in Old Delhi.

They were British, and had started in a small way after the 1939-45 war. Apparently it was by chance that they started shipping monkeys. They heard that some laboratories in Britain wanted them for research purposes, and sent a few, paying a few rupees to local catchers. The trade grew, until by now they were responsible for the export of thousands of rhesus monkeys, including a sizeable proportion of those that passed through the Hostel. Whatever my feelings about the monkey trade in general, I had to admire the way they conducted their macabre business – though much of their efficiency was probably due to the ever stricter standards imposed by the laboratories regarding the condition of the animals they were prepared to accept.

Veterinary supervision was insisted on before the animals were exported, and everything had to be done by the shippers to ensure that the animals left in prime condition. This was but one factor in the continually rising price of monkeys, which, like fish from the sea, started off in their natural state costing nothing at all. In addition, the sheer quantity of monkeys already caught had exhausted the original areas where they were found. This, sadly, was a continuing process in the steady depletion of Indian wild life. Whereas in the early fifties they could still be found just outside Delhi, less than a decade later the shippers were having to cast their nets much further afield. As in Africa, light aircraft were now used to ferry them in. This, with rising freightage and airline charges, also added to costs, so that a little rhesus monkey that would have cost about £3 when I joined the R.S.P.C.A. now had a price tag (including dealers' profits, which were not inconsiderable) nearer £100. Possibly all that had not joined the inflationary spiral was the fee of a few rupees paid to a local catcher.

With this kind of money changing hands it was a pity that equivalent high standards were not insisted on for the actual transport of the monkeys by air. This I hoped I could do something about before I left India. I was not so much concerned about big shippers, who did their best as far as crating went, but about the smaller businesses, the cowboys of the trade. I wanted my two biggest shippers to agree ideas with me that could be passed along the line.

Meanwhile I was given a guided tour of their premises, and was very impressed. They had huge cages, called 'gang-cages', out in the open, but roofed with leaves for shade, and against the downpours of the monsoon season. The cages contained anything up to a hundred or more monkeys, all looking as fit as fiddles. They were similar to cages I had seen in Nairobi, used for 'conditioning' the monkeys with plenty of food, water, and exercise, so that if there was a call from a laboratory for a consignment of a certain weight, size and sex, everything would be ready. Grading the monkeys was carried out by means of different sized wire tunnels leading to separate cages, rather like the system used at Slimbridge with wild fowl.

This was my final visit in Delhi, and as the taxi took me back out of the dust and heat to the airport, I was glad to be going. Yet I'd learned a great deal, and even extracted promises of improvement in the way the monkeys were shipped by air. I felt I might have done some good, anyway, on the theory that a personal appearance has more impact than a score of letters of protest, suggestion and indignation.

Once back at Heathrow, I was able to incorporate the information I'd gained in Nairobi, Singapore and Delhi, as well as first-hand experience of the animal freighters, into discussions that were by now being held in my office at the Hostel on the entire subject of the transport of animals by air.

We had a wide range of interested bodies: the airlines themselves, of course – B.O.A.C., B.E.A., British United, Pan-Am and so on – the British Veterinary Association, the powerful Medical Research Council, various livestock export groups including the Chick Export Association, the London Zoological Society, and the Universities Federation of Animal Welfare, as well as representatives from the packaging industry such as British Paper and Board Makers. The hope was that the British Standards Institute would incorporate all our findings into a definitive document.

And this is what happened. At last, in 1961, our work bore fruit and the B.S.I. produced a large document entitled 'Recommendations for the Carriage of Live Animals by Air'. It covered most kinds of livestock from monkeys and other primates to birds, rodents and small fur-bearing animals, as well as dogs, cats, and young poultry. It was a great step forward. The document still did not carry the force of law, of course. There was nothing mandatory about it, but at last here, in one volume, were set out the standards that represented our ideals. The Animal Charter was in being.

11

Jumbos by Jumbo

The Swinging Sixties were aptly named as far as the Hostel was concerned. From the middle to the end of the decade we were really in top gear. In one month alone at this time we dealt with a record 112,000 animals, birds, and reptiles. Our total for a year exceeded the one million mark.

This all happened as Heathrow was expanding into the true jet era. Things had really changed since the old rural days. The main runway had already been extended so that it ran past my office; it was to become, eventually, nearly three-quarters of a mile longer for the extra take-off run needed by the Boeing 707s, and later the Jumbos.

By that time, too, the centre area was being built, with the vast new terminals, the tunnel under the main runway, the approaches from the M4 and underpass at the old A4 Bath Road. With these changes there came a change in the way the livestock was handled. Instead of the monkeys, dogs, cats and so on being shunted across the A4, with great chatterings and yelpings, and in a fairly free and easy manner, we eventually had highly organized transit: from the aircraft cargo holds on to the apron, and on to the complete Cargo village where the animals would be either re-exported, or cleared by Customs, documented, and sent on to the Hostel for feeding and cleaning.

At the Hostel, the monkey trade reached and passed its peak. To deal with it and the enormously increased traffic in other animals as well, the staff numbers went up and up until we had sixteen girls. Jenny Stansfield had left to become an air hostess, and, later, to marry an airline pilot. She had quite a send-off. Among the replacements was Maureen Rew (later Faulkner), also blonde, and, like Jenny when she'd originally joined, only eighteen. Maureen was equally efficient, and was soon on her way to the top. There was also a girl called Jane who became like her namesake, Calamity Jane. She was small and full of bounce, wore her hair in a pony tail, and was very proud of being an ex-Girl Guide. But it took all her cheerfulness to meet the various dramas and minor disasters in her life at the Hostel.

I used to keep an Accident Log. Jane's entries in the years she was with us should have been entered in the *Guinness Book of Records*: 'Index finger pecked by bird. First aid given... Bitten by a mink. Tetanus injection at Port Health Centre... Clawed by an eagle...Scratched by a cat..Bitten by a dog on finger...Fingers trapped in cage doors...Overcome by chloroform while putting day-old chicks to sleep...' You name it, it happened to Jane. If anyone was trapped in a cage the rest of the girls knew who it would be... 'Mr Whittaker...it's Jane again...'

Her disasters were not limited to inside the Hostel. She used to come to work from the Ashford area on a moped, using the airfield perimeter track. Frequently, though, it seemed to break down, and she finished the final mile pushing it, arriving a red-faced, crash-helmeted figure soaked by the mist for which Heathrow is famous – but still cheerful. And she was never, breakdown or no breakdown, late for work.

From the old Bath Road the building looked much as it always had, but in nearly fifteen years the interior had seen considerable changes to meet increased traffic and changing demands. In one of the stables, for example, we had a pool, painted an attractive blue, for the release of aquatic birds and mammals: pelicans, penguins, Californian sea lions, red-eared terrapins, even giant toads. When pelicans arrived the girls would carefully open up the doors of their crates, which were just wide enough and tall enough to allow one pelican to emerge at a time. They would catch each one by the beak (making sure the pelican didn't do the grabbing first) and gently pull the bird out. Once the pelicans saw the water there was no more need for coaxing. They went into the pool with a flurry, diving up and down happily, and being fastidious, as most birds are, eagerly cleaning themselves. Sea lions were just as eager after a confined and noisy air journey, and even if our pool wasn't exactly their natural habitat it was a better approximation than a travelling crate. Terrapins would be released into the pool if their flights were delayed; once in the water, they had to be recovered by ramps and planks we lowered into the water for them. When the pool was not in use, it was turned back into a stable by covering it with boards, since space in those busy days was at a premium, so the day after pelicans had been splashing about cheerfully, the space might be occupied by racehorses, or even elephants.

One of the original rooms I'd seen on my very first day going round the Hostel back in 1952 was the Sick Bay. It was never used as such, and although for some unknown reason it never lost its title, we had turned it into a special room for tropical creatures that needed warmth. Reptiles had their own section of it. There were glass vivariums with infra-red lamps over the top that could get the temperature up to 90°F if necessary; lowering or raising the lamps varied the temperature. One reason behind keeping reptiles warm is that they refuse to feed unless the temperature is just right. In this room also we had special resuscitation cages for any birds in need, particularly sun birds or humming birds from South America or similar small birds from Africa.

These little birds are nectar feeders. Sometimes they arrived looking very distressed, even though well crated. They would be down at the bottom of the box with its polythene front, and not interested in the fountain drinker of water and glucose, or honeyed water, that had been provided for the journey. Here was further evidence of air travel being too much for such small creatures. In

147

their natural habitats they were well able to withstand quite a degree of cold at night, but exposure to flight, with all its temperature changes, was too much for them – though no dealer who was going to get £50 apiece for them seemed much worried about that!

Luckily we were always able to do something for these tiny birds; we had developed a special technique we used to revive them. The bird was taken out of the container and raised to the level of the mouth, then warm breath was exhaled until we could see its tongue slowly appearing in its beak. The next step was to bring up to the level of the bird one of our special nectar feeders. The bird, seeing the red-tipped nozzle, then used to put out its tongue, first a quarter of an inch, then half an inch, and then sip, sip, sip at the nectar solution we had made up. From that moment, recovery was only a matter of minutes away, and soon the little bird would be struggling and very much brought back to life.

Maureen proved very good at this technique. After she joined the Hostel she became more and more interested in the birds we handled; she began buying reference books, and in the end became the expert we all relied on. She usually saw to it that she was helping the unloading when we had tropical birds in.

'What are these, Maureen?'

'Look like weavers to me. Masked weavers, I think. But I'm not sure. I'll go and find out.'

She would come back with the book. '*Little* masked weaver... or *Ploceus luteola*...also called Atlas weaver, little weaver, and slender-billed weaver...common in Africa from Senegal across to Kenya...how about that?'

From black-bellied fire finches to giant East African cut-throats via Natal linnets, Cape canaries, and red-cowled cardinals, we now always got the answer when in doubt about what to fill in on the forms for a bird consignment.

In time Maureen was promoted to supervisor, in charge of all the staff, and responsible for organizing their work. I relied on her increasingly, and not just for identifying tropical birds. I left the selection of staff to her

entirely. Whether school-leavers or ex-hairdressers, sec-
retaries or girls simply fed up with working in a bank,
Maureen vetted them all before they went to R.S.P.C.A.
Headquarters hoping to be made a Probationary Hostel
Assistant. It was, I knew, Maureen's preliminary screen-
ing that ensured that we had such a marvellous lot of
helpers, devoted to the unusual work, and astonishing in
the way that they never refused any task, however
unpleasant or dangerous.

Sometimes I used to chat to Maureen about a batch of
new candidates, but I never questioned her choice.

'What were they like, Maureen?'

'One possible, I think. Two turned up their noses
when I told them about mucking out monkey cages, and
the other didn't like animals to begin with. Oh, and she
didn't like the idea of shift work, either.'

The shift work, involving night duty, and the organization of a duty roster as complicated as a school
timetable, Maureen also sorted out. Her rosters appeared
on the Hostel noticeboard every week and were full of
letters and numbers. Some letters and numbers were
more popular than others, and Maureen had to see that
girls didn't get lumbered two weeks running.

Depending on what was in, the export kennels were
not a bad number, but it needed a sharp eye to make sure
the wrong dog didn't get into the wrong box and end up
on the other side of the world with the wrong owner: our
equivalent of passenger in Paris, baggage in Bogotá .
Quarantine kennels, watching that all the strict precautions, particularly against rabies, were observed, could
be a chore. What was certainly not top of the pops was
duty in the tropical fish room. We were quite proud of
the room and its facilities, but it made for deadly boring
and hard work handling tens of thousands of tropical fish
a year. It was mainly re-oxygenating the plastic bags
containing fish in transit, and had to be carried out in
semi-darkness and in a temperature up to ninety degrees.
Occasionally the routine would be enlivened – though
I'm not sure that's quite the word– by a consignment of
Australian lung fish that had chewed their way through

their heavy-duty plastic bags. They would be re-pack-aged, and then immediately start chewing their way out again.

No wonder the girls preferred a spell of duty in the stables, which might contain their favourite 'baby ellies' – baby elephants – or, equally popular, racehorses. We used to get quite a few racehorses staying round about the time of the Cheltenham Festival in March, invariably part of the mass Irish invasion when they seemed to win most of the races. The girls always hoped that by some miracle they would come in one morning, and find Arkle, the greatest steeplechaser of them all, in one of the boxes. But it never happened.

Nor, to my knowledge, did we ever have a winner through the Hostel. Though it wasn't for want of support by the girls. Particularly Jane. During Chel-tenham Festival time you could set your watch by the sound of her moped chugging away during the dinner hour into the distance in the direction of the betting shop in Hillingdon. She would come back beaming and excited.

'What's the big tip today, Jane?'

'I didn't know you were a betting man, Mr Whittaker.'

'I'm not. I just want to know so I can stop anyone else backing it.'

Sure enough, come the results, there would be no mention of our Hostel horse. If the Girl Guides had awarded badges for losing on horses Jane would have had an armful of them.

About this time the monkey trade began to decline. We had already handled, since we started operations, an incredible half a million monkeys. But from the height of the traffic, when the big Super-Constellation freighters were employing more than a dozen 'monkey men', the trade began to tail off as the laboratories manufacturing polio vaccine began to use tissue instead of kidneys. There was also a natural falling off after the first big vaccination programmes had been carried out, and public opposition to vaccination further reduced manu-facture, and hence the call for monkeys.

At the same time we were well into the jet age and it was not long before the Jumbos came on the scene. These effectively put an end to the animal freighters because they could take big cargoes of livestock in their great holds, immediately reducing journey times and cutting down the stress and strain. It was the biggest single advance on behalf of animals since the first one travelled by air. We were into the age of Jumbos by Jumbo.

It was possibly just as well. One of the last freighters into Heathrow with a cargo of elephants met with one of the oddest bits of misfortune in airline history. It was carrying Indian elephants, smaller and less wild than their African cousins, but with great tusks and flapping ears. I had a call to go to the aircraft, and arrived on the tarmac as the first elephant was being unloaded. But this wasn't what caught my eye. I looked at the freighter, and saw liquid spilling from it, over the unloading ramp. It looked quite a big fuel or hydraulic leak. 'I wonder if they know,' I thought. 'Ought I to tell somebody?' Then one of the freight handlers caught sight of me.

'Hello R.S.P.C.A.,' he said, and broke into a grin, 'we've got a job on here. Go and have a look.'

I could hear a trumpeting from inside the fuselage, and thought that the elephants must be giving trouble, so I went up the ramp to see what I could do. I was just about to step inside when, with a reflex action, I drew my foot back from the threshold. As I did so, and the wild trumpeting went on from within, I realized that this was not just the Call of the Wild, but the Call of Nature as well. On elephant scale. The deck of the freighter was awash. In all the years of freighting animals nothing like it had ever happened before. Luckily all I had to do was see the elephants themselves were O.K., which they were, and on arrival in the Hostel they couldn't have been better behaved.

Perhaps it was better travelling conditions, perhaps shorter flight times, I don't know, but there was never a repetition of this once the Jumbos starting operating. We had a great number of elephants staying with us for shorter or longer times. The favourite out of them all, and the one who stayed longest – so much so that she became a Hostel pet – was Tanya.

Tanya you might really call a royal elephant. She had appeared before H.M. the Queen at a Royal Command Variety Performance. She was a feature of Palladium shows, appearing with Dickie Henderson, when she used to do the rumba, an activity she considered very much beneath her dignity. Normally our maximum for a stay at the Hostel was forty-eight hours, but one day we had a wire urgently requesting extended accommodation for Tanya, whose permanent quarters at the Palladium were not ready. So, for this famous elephant, we bent the rules, and never regretted it.

She had been appearing at the Tiergarten, Berlin, and arrived one evening with Smahar, her trainer. The truck arrived at the Hostel, the back was let down, and we had our first glimpse of the friendliest but also the biggest elephant we'd ever seen. Tanya was *huge*. Weightwatchers would have have made a fortune out of her. But, big or not, she was nimble. The leather-covered chain restrainers were unshackled and at one word of command from Smahar she backed her great bulk down the ramp as neatly as a ballet dancer. No wonder she could do the rumba.

Another word of command, and Tanya gave us all, Hostel staff, loaders, and driver, a bow. Then she placidly walked through the main hall with Smahar to the quarters we'd got ready with four bales of hay and a full water trough. We'd hoped this would be to her liking, and any doubts disappeared as soon as Tanya got inside her stable. Her trunk went up, and she gave a terrific trumpet of pleasure. A moment later she was draining the trough and starting in on the hay.

From then on she was one of the family. We fed her hay with bran and oats, and, because it was autumn, mixed in some ginger for warmth against the English weather. After her morning feed came the bit we all liked best: bath-time. Tanya used to come out of her loose-box and, at one word of command, lie down and roll over for her elephant version of the Toilet of Venus. The girls had scrubbing brushes and buckets of water, and Tanya used to love it; she splashed about, waving her legs and thinking perhaps that it mightn't be an Indian river but it was the next best thing. She would let them do anything with her, even sit on her tummy; it was amazing that such an immense creature could be so docile.

After that, the morning routine took a less decorous turn. We used to let Tanya out into the paddock for a short while to stretch her legs – not for too long because the October mornings were beginning to be rather nippy, but long enough for the inevitable result of a good meal, rolling about in the bath, and taking exercise. And if Tanya with her great size may not quite have been able to move mountains, she could certainly produce them.

Shifting what might have become an entire mountain

range presented us with problems. Then I had a brainwave. 'I know what,' I said to Maureen, 'we'll use a
wheelbarrow.'

Maureen looked slightly perplexed. 'But we already
use a wheelbarrow.'

'No, no,' I said, 'what I mean is, if one of the girls takes
a wheelbarrow out when Tanya goes into the paddock,
then she can follow Tanya around, and as soon as...'

I didn't get any further. Maureen was not reacting very
seriously to my inspiration.

I went on patiently, 'What I mean is, it'll save a lot of
work if we catch it first...'

Which made Maureen even less serious. Still, I suppose
they laughed at Einstein when he discovered relativity. I
know that genius often goes unrecognized. Eventually
Maureen calmed down enough to agree it wasn't a bad
idea.

So, every morning from then on, when Tanya ambled
out for her constitutional, she was closely attended by
one of the girls solemnly trundling immediately behind
with a wheelbarrow, ever alert for signs that the Great
Movement was about to take place. After that, it was a
matter of deftly shunting the barrow into place, standing
back, and letting nature and gravity join forces. Everyone agreed the idea was a success in reducing what might
be called the Hostel work-load.

At the time of Tanya's stay, a film was being made at
Heathrow called *The Airport Story*. The Hostel was
featured in it, and having such a highly trained elephant
on the guest-list gave the film-makers a chance they
didn't want to miss. Accordingly, one marvellous sequence shows Tanya walking into our admin block, past
Reception, and knocking with her trunk on my office
door. The door opens, and there is a shot of her just
managing to squeeze in and wave her trunk over my
desk. I'm sitting behind it with three apples ready in a
drawer. She takes the apples in turn, and, having seen
where they come from, tries to delve her trunk into the
drawer I say 'No more, Tanya', and she obediently
backs out with immense dignity.

Without any doubt, Tanya was the best-loved elephant we ever had at the Hostel, and we were all sorry when the time came for her to move into her permanent Palladium quarters. She came back for short stays on a couple of occasions, and each time got the royal welcome she deserved from us. But then we lost track of her until I heard, years later, what had happened to her. Apparently she had continued to put on weight until it was too expensive for Smahar to air-freight her round the world. She ended up eventually in a pleasure park in America, and there she died. We were all very, very sad at the news, and just hoped that she'd come to the end of her life with the dignity and happiness that were so much part of her when we knew her.

If Tanya was the most popular elephant we'd ever had, the one that took the prize at the other end of the scale, and really through no fault of his own, was Little Babar. Little Babar came in one night when all the stables where we would normally put elephants were full. It happened that doing her stint on night duty was Jane, our little ex-Guide with two left feet and a heart of gold.

When Little Babar was unloaded and brought into the Hostel round about 2 a.m., Jane realized that some initiative would be needed to find a place for him. She happily took up the challenge. She found the very place for him, outside one of the stables which were stacked high with crates of birds in for one single night. These crates, and those in the other stables, were stacked on top of the big iron ring-bolts that had been specially let into the floor for tethering elephants and other big creatures. So here was a further problem, and a further chance for Jane's initiative to shine. No ring-bolts, but Little Babar had to be secured. Where? thought Jane, looking round. The bars on the stables, perhaps? This would have kept him nicely in check. But no. Jane had a better idea. There were the radiators, with convenient piping running from ceiling to floor. In a twinkling there was a hitch of the kind that earned Jane promotion in the Guides, and Little Babar was tethered to the pipes.

A job well done, and Jane was soon making her way

back along the passage towards a cuppa in the staff kitchen. Little Babar saw her going, and, being a friendly soul, decided to follow. There was an accompanying creak. Then a slight groaning. Followed by the noise of fracturing. Jane turned and stood transfixed. Little Babar, waving his trunk in the friendliest possible way, was advancing on her, accompanied by immense sounds of wrenching, and finally, with the radiator adrift from its moorings and being dragged along the floor, a great crashing of plaster falling as pipes came away, closely followed by a torrent of water bursting from the ceiling...Little Babar didn't even notice. Now Jane had stopped he was happy to call it a day. He stood right under the cascade of water, and enjoyed the free bath.

Poor Jane. She was in tears when I arrived not long afterwards in response to a panic phone call from her. We managed to turn the water off, and I surveyed the damage. It was clear that Little Babar had wrecked practically the entire central heating system. I turned to Jane.

'Never mind,' I said, 'it wasn't your fault. One big winner, and we can pay for this lot.'

12

Great Snakes

In the earlier days at the Hostel the routine for getting on to the airport itself was practically non-existent. Things were very informal. I could meet, say, a Constellation, or one of the old Vikings, and simply walk aboard. The captains were usually very friendly, and if there were passengers in transit who were flying on to another destination in the aircraft I would check to see if they had any animals because some airlines, such as Pan-Am and Air India, allowed animals to be carried in the cabin, at the captain's discretion. If any other transit passengers had a dog or cat they were always delighted to see the R.S.P.C.A. because we could feed, water, and exercise their pets for them while they waited.

But in time, and with the eruption of violence into world events, security became very strict. We had to have identity tags, with photographs, even to get on the tarmac, let alone to board a Jumbo. Obviously, with the growth of terrorism and bomb-scares, it was necessary. But one incident, while proving that it's better not to take chances with possible terrorism, had an unexpected ending.

Once again I was alerted by signal. An aircraft had landed in Sweden with a bomb-scare. All the baggage was taken out of the hold, the hold was searched, and each piece of luggage was checked on the apron where it had been put, well away from the aircraft and airport buildings. No bomb was found. But one suitcase for some reason proved suspicious. It was opened up, and inside was a linen bag. Not only that, but the linen bag was moving. Obviously not a bomb, at least. But what was it? No one was particularly keen on finding out, so the bag was put back in the suitcase, and passengers, now the check was complete, were asked to reclaim their cases and holdalls. Every piece of baggage was reclaimed, and sent on to the hold – except one: the suitcase with the mysterious moving linen bag in it!

There followed a further crisis of indecision. No one wanted to have anything to do with it. There were no facilities at the airport, anyway, for dealing with creatures in transit in this peculiar way. Then someone had a bright idea: send it on, unopened, to Heathrow. The Animal Hostel could cope, and, to be on the safe side, a signal could be telexed.

So the airliner duly arrived. I was waiting, and personally took charge of the strange suitcase. We took it back to the Hostel, and there, with a great deal of curiosity, opened up first the case, and then the linen bag, which, indeed, was moving before our very eyes.

I pulled the cord from the neck of the bag, and out came...a snake! It was a very beautiful creature, of a variety I'd never seen before, and couldn't even identify: about five feet in length (no wonder the bag moved), indigo-black in colour, and with a gloss on it like patent leather. We put it into one of our vivariums, and then came the problem of what to do with it. The Customs came down in the inevitable shape of Old Crusty and a young assistant. They peered at it this way and that. They examined the linen bag. They looked into every corner of the case. Finally there was a pronouncement.

'Unclaimed property, mate,' said Old Crusty in his usual charming, blunt way, 'unclaimed property, that's what it is.' And they marched out.

So, since the Customs weren't interested, it seemed to be our snake. We kept it in luxury for some time before eventually finding a zoo to take it, but we never solved the mystery of what it was doing in its linen bag, and why no one claimed it. Most probably, whoever owned it hadn't had a licence to import it but had hoped to smuggle the snake in. Put off by the bomb-scare check in Sweden, they must then have decided to abandon it, and not involve themselves. So they lost an unusual and handsome pet.

Not so handsome – in fact, extremely sinister-looking and ugly – was another snake, a Gaboon viper who came to us by accident rather than design. The Gaboon viper is not an aggressive snake, but if it does strike the venom is extremely dangerous and powerful. So when I had a message that a Gaboon viper was on its way to us (somehow the documentation was out of order, and there was no entry permit for the country it was destined for), I wasn't very keen on keeping it for long.

I got in touch with the reptile people at London Zoo, and spoke to my friend David Ball, Overseer of Reptiles. I explained what had happened. They were delighted, and said they would love to have the snake. Nevertheless, it still had to be kept overnight at the Hostel. I very carefully supervised its unloading into the vivarium, with infra-red heating. It was certainly no oil painting and, although very lethargic, it was extremely large and monstrously thick in the girth. Not a pretty sight, I thought, as I turned off the outside light and left our Gaboon viper to slumber under the infra-red.

Next morning, when I came on duty, I learned the reason why the unwanted guest looked as it did. Maureen rushed up to me as soon as I arrived. 'What do you think?' she said, 'The Gaboon viper's given birth during the night: she's had nineteen babies!'

It was a maternity case I could have done without. The junior version of the Gaboon viper is certainly tinier, and, marginally, not quite so ugly, but its venom is equally powerful and toxic. So now I had sixteen (four had died) potential dangers on my hands. I rang London Zoo again and told them: 'This is your lucky day. You're not getting just one Gaboon viper, you're getting sixteen.'

They seemed even more thrilled than when I had rung the previous day, and later that morning took receipt of their new exhibits. The story ended rather sadly, though.

The following day David Ball rang to say the Gaboon viper had given birth to yet another lot of babies, but she had died soon afterwards.

This was not the only dangerous snake we entertained, by any means. Going forward a little to a time just before I retired, an airliner came in from South Africa, and it was found that some of the baggage had been broken into, including a large holdall inside which was found a leopard tortoise – a very large variety – and, in a pocket at the side, a glass jar containing a tiger snake. Whoever had been attempting to steal from the bag obviously found far more (and, of course, in another sense, rather less) than they had bargained for. Scattered around the holdall, in the aircraft's baggage compartment, were the rest of the contents, consisting of several smallish hessian sacks. Altogether, it must have been a sharp lesson that crime, at that attempt anyway, didn't pay.

This had all been found by the staff cleaning out the baggage compartment on arrival at Heathrow, and they, like the would-be thief or thieves, didn't very much like what they saw. So, naturally, they were out of the baggage hold fairly smartly, and via their supervisor the phone was soon ringing at the Hostel. Because it was the evening, I had gone off duty, and so the three who were on night shift went to deal with the mystery of the sacks, as well as the leopard tortoise and tiger snake.

So they collected the holdall and the hessian sacks. By the time they arrived back at the Hostel they knew by the feel of the sacks that they contained snakes, so they went straight to the vivariums, switched on the infra-red lamps, and prepared to empty the sacks.

To do this, one of the girls, Janice, held a metal grille (not the actual lid of the vivarium) that slid over the top, so that as the sack was shaken out very gently into the vivarium the live contents could, without danger and with no risk of escape, be put inside.

I had taught this safety routine, and it was just as well I had, because as Janice held the grille, and Kerry and Jackie gently took the first sack, lowered it equally gently into the top of the vivarium, and quickly pulled the knot apart, out slithered a puff adder! Then another, and another, all hissing, puffing, and blowing angrily as they dropped, coiling and uncoiling, to the bottom of the vivarium.

The girls were, literally, horror-struck. The puff adder is, of all snakes, one of the most dangerous: a horse bitten by one dies within a few hours, and the effect on human beings is correspondingly quicker. African tribesmen apparently used to tip their arrows with the poison of the puff adder. There was only one consolation: at least these were not fully grown to their adult 6-foot length. But it didn't make the situation any the less scary or dangerous. There was a sigh of relief as the hessian sack was unceremoniously dropped into the vivarium on top of the writhing, deadly occupants, the grille quickly removed, and the lid slammed shut.

But this was only the beginning, as the girls, nothing daunted, picked up the second hessian sack. The routine was followed as before, but, if anything, with even greater care. It was just as well, for as Jackie took a turn with the grille, and Janice quickly unknotted the sack, out fell a twisting heap of another highly dangerous variety, and in greater numbers than out of the first bag. This time they were spitting cobras, and, true to their nature, they were spitting their poison from the second they were released. So much so that the venom ran down the sides of the vivarium as, once again, the lid was whipped into its slots and secured. The girls here again very much thanked their training for not opening the sacks and having a look first. The spitting cobra, a variety that also comes from Africa, from Mozambique up to Eqypt, is a violent and aggressive reptile. It can eject posion from its mouth to a distance of several feet, and almost always aims at the eyes of any animal or human within range.

By this time, Maureen was on duty as well, and she decided to phone me at home. I arrived just as they were about to tackle the remaining two bags. I was greeted by a rather nervous joke. 'How about this for surprise packets?' said Jackie. As she said it, however, I couldn't help noticing how white-faced she and the others were. And I soon saw with what good reason. I felt my heart turn over as I looked at the undulating heaps in the first two vivariums, and, at the same time, a blind anger at the sheer irresponsibility of whoever had decided to smuggle this lethal cargo, which, compounded by the greed of a would-be thief, had put the lives of these girls at risk.

We turned to the final two hessian sacks. After what had happened so far there could hardly be worse to follow. As it turned out, there was a third variety of highly dangerous snake in them, boomslangs – with the added complication that some were dead, so we had the problem of separating them from the living ones – a final straw to a dangerous and unnecessary night's work.

It all resulted in a court case against the shippers – but also a much happier ending. Maureen Faulkner, Janice Keefe, Kerry Brodie and Jackie Fenlon all received very much deserved R.S.P.C.A. awards for bravery. They were presented at the Society's Annual General Meeting at the Café Royal in London by Dr Coggan, then Archbishop of Canterbury, and the event was given great coverage by television and Press – all of which was some compensation for the girls who had not, as they could so easily have done, shirked the entire task when they realized what great danger it involved.

One further snake story, but from the earlier days of the Hostel, when there was rather more night flying at Heathrow than is permitted today. A Constellation had come into the circuit just after midnight with an emergency. It was having difficulty getting its wheels down.

At just before 2 a.m. I had a phone call from the Control Tower. Would I come as quickly as possible. 'There's a Connie in the circuit that's got a problem you'll have to deal with when it lands – if it lands, that is.'

'What sort of problem?' I asked, half-asleep, and totally unable to see what I could do to help.

'There's a snake round the undercarriage lever,' I was told, and the phone went dead.

That jerked me into life. Peg was awake by now as well, and when I told her what was happening said, sensibly, 'But what do they expect you to do?'

To that I really had no answer at all, but I dressed and got down to the airport as quickly as I could, driving straight down to the tarmac. There was a group of freight handlers, airline officials, and other odd bodies out there, one of whom said, when he saw me approaching, 'Now, here's the very man.'

But no one seemed to think it much of a joke. We could hear the aircraft, and we could only hazard guesses at the panic that must be going on up there. 2.30 a.m. came and went. Then 3 a.m. Still the Constellation orbited. 'He can't have all that much fuel left,' said someone.

Then, just as everyone was preparing for a real emergency – a wheels-up landing – we heard the engine note change. The landing lights came on, and we saw the Constellation on the approach. A few minutes later it touched down, everyone breathed again, and at 3.23 precisely it taxied on to the hard-standing in front of us in the floodlights. The engines were cut and windmilled to a stop, leaving a silence on the chilly night air in which we could hear the doors being unlocked. At the cockpit window we could see the face of the captain looking, in the lights, very white and very unsmiling.

The steps were wheeled out. The doors opened, and I was first up and through. An air hostess greeted me as if nothing had happened. 'R.S.P.C.A? Would you go straight to the flight-deck please.'

The captain was still in his seat, but, the emergency over, regaining composure by the minute. 'Ah. R.S.P.C.A. We could have done with you…there he is…he's all yours.'

He indicated with his foot among the mass of dials, buttons and levers that I could dimly see in the low cockpit lighting. There, just, I could make out the snake. He looked to be asleep.

'I think he's asleep.'

'I think so, too. If he hadn't been, we wouldn't be here.'

'No,' I said, not really understanding, and deciding I'd better get him into the basket I'd brought as soon as possible. I bent forward, put out a hand, grabbed him quickly, and, before he could get out of my grasp and really come awake, got him into the basket and closed the lid. In the moment I was lowering 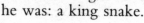 him in I recognized what kind he was: a king snake.

'Well done,' said the captain, 'it was a hairy do. Many thanks.'

Then I got the story of what happened. 'We couldn't believe it. We were just going to lower the undercart and saw this thing. It was incredible. How it got in from the hold I'll never know. But it was just in behind the undercarriage lever, and we couldn't possibly select undercarriage down with it there. So we had to orbit and hope it would move.'

'What did the passengers think?'

'They took it pretty well. We gave them free drinks. Told them there were operational problems that we'd soon sort out, and didn't mention snakes at all!'

'How did you manage to get in then?'

'Well, it did move eventually, but not very far, and no one was very keen on going near it.'

'So you hoped it would go to sleep?'

'I reckoned it might because it was quite near the cockpit heating duct. And it did. And here we are – touch wood.'

'A bit of luck,' I said.

'A bit of luck,' said the captain.

With that I said goodnight and made my way out of the cockpit, through the empty aircraft and down the steps with the cause of all the panic safe in my basket. There was one thing, though, that I didn't have the heart to tell the captain. The king snake is a completely harmless species.

13

Feeding Time

So we had our elephant problems. But one thing about the elephants that was in inverse proportion to their size was the problem of feeding them. Baby elephants were thus more trouble than their fully-grown parents. We fed them on evaporated milk, and sometimes it needed a lot of patience to get them to take it. In addition we made up rice and bran into lumps the size and shape of tennis balls, lifted their little trunks, and popped them in. The baby elephants took them like human children downing Maltesers.

For grown elephants we provided sugar beet and cane for their feeding in flight, and to conserve this while they were with us we supplemented their rations with new-mown grass whenever we could. Here we were lucky that we lived on an airfield the size of Heathrow. Contractors used to mow the grass between the runways at regular intervals. The grass was then delivered to a pellet factory on the perimeter of the airfield to be processed and sold as animal feed. We always tried to get in a stage ahead of the processing. When we had elephants staging through at the right time of year I would take down some empty sacks in the Land-Rover, and usually I was lucky enough to be able to fill up, at the cost of a few shillings, with the sweet-smelling, delicious, new-mown grass. The elephants loved it, waving their trunks for more when we fed it to them.

Altogether, catering for the airborne menagerie constantly on the move through our doors meant we had to be able to provide menus as varied as the Savoy Grill, although one item we stocked in our deep-freeze beat anything the Savoy could provide: powdered deep-frozen mouse for feeding to snakes. Not for the squeamish. When we didn't stock whatever was required it was never much trouble to go and get it. So when Benji the gorilla arrived for a brief stay, with quite explicit feeding instructions on his box, Maureen was despatched into Hillingdon for his choice of food: punnet after punnet of strawberries, which disappeared without a hint of appreciation of the lengths we'd gone to for his palate.

But, however much we tried, we couldn't always cope, and this was the case with Fifi, a Pekinese. Fifi was the most pampered and cosseted dog I have ever come across. She had been owned by a wealthy couple in the Bahamas who had died. They left Fifi to their nurse Maria, an Austrian girl, with the stipulation that the Peke was to have the very best veterinary treatment in the world should she need it. More than enough money, in addition, was left to provide for air travel both for Fifi and Maria. So, one day, we were treated to the sight of a Peke arriving in an airline-crew car. Fifi may have been travelling under Ministry Quarantine Licence, but she did it in style, perched grandly on a pink satin cushion, with the entire back of the car to herself.

This, I learned, was nothing to the space she'd commanded on the flight over from the Bahamas. In the front was Maria, who came over to my office to discuss arrangements for the dog. Fifi was apparently suffering with her teeth, and was *en route* under quarantine all the way to Hackbridge Kennels for treatment. But she would be in our quarantine kennels for forty-eight hours.

We came to the question of food. I began to explain the kind of bill of fare that Fifi might expect at the Hostel when Maria politely cut me short. 'No, no,' she said, 'don't worry. It's all been taken care of. The Aerial Hotel will provide the food, and you can charge it on the bill.'

The Aerial Hotel is on the perimeter of the airfield, and, pausing only to wonder how a dog with toothache who had travelled several thousand miles to have it put right would cope with hotel food – or even needed to – I despatched one of the girls.

She reported to the hotel manager who, standing by for the summons for 'Maria's dog's dinner', solemnly called the chef. The chef, equally solemnly, said what he personally recommended, and the girl came back with Chicken Kiev. The following day there was Boeuf Stroganov for lunch, followed in the evening by Agneau Roti Aerial Hotel. On each occasion Fifi deigned to leave the pink satin cushion on which she sat resplendent in our quarantine kennels, and dealt, without manners to match, with her three-star meals.

But the incident was not without some reward. Maria, not bound by quarantine regulations, made the most of her time shopping in the West End, and, on Fifi's final evening, took Peg and me to the Aerial Hotel, where we had a magnificent dinner. For ever after that I was able to say with truth, when people asked about what we fed the dogs at the Hostel: 'They eat just as well as we do – and vice versa.'

After arranging Boeuf Stroganov for a dog, and strawberries for a gorilla, it might seem that life could present few more surprises when it came to feeding animals. But how do you feed ant-eaters if you've no ants? This one really stretched our ingenuity to the full. The first time we had a consignment of these inoffensive animals, with their great long, tapering snouts, and strange flickering long tongues, coated with stickiness to scoop up their natural food from the great ant-hills they prey on, I recalled something I had once read about them. It was *The Narrative of a Voyage to Surinam*, and the author recounted how the natives of this island in the (then) Dutch East Indies used to call the little ant-eater that lived there 'Kissing Hand': 'The inhabitants pretend that it will never eat, at least when caught, but that it only licks its paws, in the same manner as the bear; that all trials to make it eat have proved in vain, and that it soon dies in confinement.'

So, I thought, we had a problem. At least the ant-eaters had not died in confinement. But as for ants, if we could have found any in the paddock there would probably not have been enough to keep one of them going for more than a fraction of a day. And, it struck me, British ants might not be to their taste anyway.

So the girls and I had a conference. Maureen was in favour of trying minced meat, chopped very fine. The ant-eaters, as we brought the dishes out to them, sat securely in their boxes, peering at us with their very small but not unkind eyes. We put the minced meat up to their boxes, put samples on our fingers, and finally coaxed them out, being careful of their claws, which are used to dig out ants' nests. They studied the minced meat carefully and approached it from varying angles, but not an ant-eater would touch the food. They simply weren't interested. We had to think of something else.

The next suggestion was evaporated milk. We went through the entire routine again. Not a flicker of enthusiasm. Each ant-eater, metaphorically anyway, turned up its long, elegant snout.

I then had an idea. In my mind I could already see the ant-eaters wasting away. 'We could put out a radio appeal,' I said, 'and ask people to dig up ants' nests and bring them here.'

But at the same time Jane, not noted for brainwaves, but who had been cogitating on the fringe of the discussion group, came up with a suggestion. 'Why,' she said, with the sort of look in her eyes I imagine scientists have when they split atoms, or worse, 'don't we do some more chopped mince...*and* mix it with evaporated milk...*and* an egg?'

The effect was a bit like that old ad. for Home Piano Tutors: 'They laughed when I sat down to play, but when they heard me perform Beethoven's Moonlight Sonata, their laughter turned to amazement...' We had to give it a try. So, back to the chopping board, and eventually, led by a confident Jane, out came the bowls again. The ant-eaters once again were coaxed from their boxes. They shuffled round the bowls, putting their snouts in. Was I mistaken, or was there at least a flicker of interest? No one said a word. Then we saw first one ant-eater, then another, start eating. In the end all six of them were eagerly eating up their substitute food, their long tongues darting out and in, until every bowl was clean. Jane, quite rightly, was beside herself with pleasure, and we were all pleased for her, too.

But the ant-eaters were not the only ones who had unusual tastes that somehow had to be satisfied. The arrival of a consignment of leaf-eating monkeys, with instructions on their boxes for feeding, caused yet another dietary conference among the staff, and the eventual departure of two of the girls and me in the Land-Rover to Cranford Woods, about three miles away, in search of oak leaves. We saw the keeper and explained what was wanted, and he told us to help ourselves. I looked around, and said, 'Just what we want.' I got a strange look from the keeper.

'They're sycamores,' he said drily, and with the

slightest hint of contempt. Pointing in the other direction he said 'There's the oaks. I'd better take you.'

I know I've never been any good at tree identification, so, realizing my ignorance might have had serious consequences for the leaf-eating monkeys, I trusted the keeper, and we filled the Land-Rover with enough oak leaves to keep the monkeys happy until they departed.

The squirrel monkeys from South America eat fruit as a main part of their diet. These were the little olive green monkeys that were first into space; the Americans, for some reason I could never fathom, called them Cain and Abel. They also eat vegetables and bread. But the thing they have to have in addition is live food in the not very attractive shape of meal worms. By the time I left the Hostel, these were becoming very expensive indeed, up to 75p an ounce. We would have boxes of meal worms flown in at £7 a time mostly from West Germany, and the squirrel monkeys used to relish them, all unaware of the Ritz-type price of their menu.

A less exotic kind of worm was required for some of the birds we had through: these were common, and literally garden, earthworms. Which, it might be thought, would present no difficulty. But, although everyone has seen thrushes and blackbirds on a lawn stopping and listening for underground movement of worms and deftly pulling them out of the turf, human beings are not so well equipped for this sort of thing.

However, after we had scoured the paddock and found no more than three unsuspecting worms by digging, the girls once again came up with an idea. They decided to get some sacking, soak it in gravy, and leave it in the paddock overnight. It worked. I was called out the following morning: 'Come and look at this, Mr Whittaker.'

There was Maureen, holding the sacking, and proudly pointing to what amounted to a banquet of worms. These were gathered before they could disappear, and were much appreciated by the birds (and later, when we used the same methods, by some of the amphibians).

Although collecting earthworms the way we did

wasn't perhaps the most pleasant of tasks, it was nothing to the unpleasantness – for want of a better word – associated with the feeding of some creatures that require live food. One day we had a shipment of flycatchers and bee-eaters in. They had live locusts in their feeding boxes, which might sound fine, bearing in mind that this was their natural food; indeed, it might appear that the shipper had been unusually thoughtful. In one way, I suppose he had. But he had also been quite cynically cruel. Every locust, as well as some grasshoppers, had had its wings and legs pulled off to stop it escaping.

This was nothing to a collection of leopards that flew in one day from India. When we examined their boxes – rather carefully, because these animals can't be trusted – I was surprised to see in the corner of one of the first boxes, crouching in the furthest spot from the leopard they could find, two emerald doves. When I examined the box more closely the reason became clear. The floor of the crate was strewn with the remains of the other doves; they had been put in live to provide food on the journey.

When we discovered this cruelty, I at once took steps through the R.S.P.C.A. to have the appalling practice stopped. Eventually it was, but not before many more shipments of leopards and similar large cats had come in with grisly mementoes of in-flight meals: a sad spectrum of birds who deserved a better fate, including ring-necked parakeets, blossom-neck parakeets, and mynah birds which, even then (had the profit-minded shippers known it, they wouldn't have been on the list), were fetching £10 – £15 a time.

King penguins are birds that require a particular kind of feeding procedure; we were lucky to have someone to show us how to do it the first time this species came to the Hostel, destined for Smart's Circus. The king penguin, next to the emperor, is the biggest of all the penguins, and far larger than any penguins we had ever handled – such as the little rock-hoppers, which we had in dozens. King penguins are over two feet tall, and handsomely marked. Unlike the smaller penguins, they feed under-water, and this facility we were unable to provide,

173

because our pool was too shallow. Billy Smart's son told us they could be hand-fed instead. We had already taken from our deep-freeze a pack of frozen herring of the kind kept on hand for when sea-lions came through (whom we used to feed through a hole in their transit cages), and Billy Smart's son came along to demonstrate.

There were just over twenty king penguins, all indicating that they were hungry, when he arrived. 'What you want to do, girls,' he said, 'is this', and, herring at the ready, he demonstrated. When he had successfully fed the first one, I was glad that he had addressed the girls – ungallant as it may sound – and not included me. The procedure consisted of getting a hand under the penguin's neck, clamping the wings with the knees, and with the other hand opening the beak and forcing the herring down the penguin's throat.

The girls blenched a little as they watched, but, game as ever, tackled the job with immense zest, and, I may say, demonstrated quite literally that they were not the weaker sex. The king penguins are strong creatures, and, despite realizing that this was feeding time, gave a performance that would not have looked amiss on I.T.V.'s All-in Wrestling spot. They waddled about, jumped up and down, and flapped their wings; it took all the girls' nerve to deal with them. They certainly needed their rubber aprons and wellingtons – as well as energy.

But the king penguins were not the most troublesome creatures the team had to deal with. This doubtful honour belongs to the baby bears we frequently had in large numbers from the Himalayas. In their case, it was sheer exuberance and immaturity that caused the problems: certainly not their size, for, poor little things, they were hardly weaned from their mothers, and scarcely bigger than three-month-old labrador puppies. They were fed with hot milk, cereal, bread and honey, all mixed together. They would rush the food, and fight over it, and once again the girls were in the thick of a fight, this time more like referees in all-in wrestling, separating the contestants.

Bees we had in thousands when the hive population

was diminished in this country by heavy rain and bad weather, causing poor pollination conditions. To replenish, a strain of bees was imported from Italy, and it was during this period that we had a signal from an Alitalia airliner. Bees were reported escaping from the hold. The aircraft was due within half an hour, and there was a request for the R.S.P.C.A. to meet it.

It didn't say how many bees had escaped, or what part of the aircraft they were in. But it could be serious if enough had found their way to the flight-deck, and unpleasant even if they were only in the passenger compartments. By the time I'd loaded up the ambulance with nets and protective gauze, and asked Maureen to get two of the girls – but to warn them what they were in for – my mind was working overtime picturing what might be happening at 20,000 feet over Sussex or Surrey...

... the cockpit was swarming with bees...the instrument panel crawling with them, so the dials couldn't be seen...the pilot was fending off bees with one arm and trying to keep one hand firm on the controls...the crew were fighting to keep them off him...back in the cabin there was panic and confusion...passengers were being stung and were on their feet and in the aisles trying to get away from the bees and affecting the trim of the aircraft and making it buck and yaw all over the sky...the pilot was appealing over the address system for them to keep calm and be seated again...

...the aircraft had made it to the crucial last-minute adjustments on the approach...the bees were still swarming...undercarriage and flaps down...the pilot is stung...but carries on...500 feet...400 feet...the pilot is stung again...there's nothing he can do, he has to keep both hands on the controls and both feet on the rudder bar...300 feet...nearly there...ready to ease back for the landing...then the pilot is stung again...and again...he passes out...one of the crew tries to get control...but too late...the aircraft on the last hundred feet spins to the runway out of control...

This picture, with variations, ran itself over and over again in my mind. Until, taxi-ing along towards us, looking perfectly normal, we saw an airliner. It was turning on the hard-standing, Alitalia plainly on its side, not a sign that anything might be wrong. So much for imagination. When it had stopped and the doors opened, we donned the protective clothing, grabbed our nets, and went on board. Fortunately the bees were in the hold and only a few had got in to the cabin, though the passengers were getting off as quickly as possible. We managed to catch most of the bees, but it wasn't possible to get them all. In my pocket I'd brought an aerosol can. I didn't want to use it, but it was a last resort. We had to get rid of the last of the bees that way. Finally the aircraft was clear.

Meanwhile the cause of all the trouble was being unloaded and the loaders were the worst plagued – so much so that it was some time before they could unload the Royal Mail. The bees travelled by air in special frames with gauze fronts, which made a sort of two-dimensional mini-hive, with the queen in a little plastic box at the centre. That ensured the rest of the hive population stayed put. That was the theory, anyway. In fact two of the frames had shifted in the hold while in transit and the gauze had broken. And the queen bee theory hadn't worked. We had two empty frames, and two lonely queen bees.

The rest of the intact frames were shifted over to the ambulance, and we took them back to the Hostel. Having off-loaded the bees there would be a delay until cargo manifests were amended and other documents raised. Hence we would have to feed the bees. But how?

I contacted the importers, who had already been warned by Alitalia about what had happened. 'Is there any special food?' I asked. There wasn't, apparently. 'Just granulated sugar dissolved in water,' they said.

It sounded simple enough. But then came the snag. How did we feed the bees their sugar solution? After a great deal of chat we decided the best way was to spray the front of the 'hives'. But with what? The answer came from Maureen.

'Flit guns,' she said.

'But we haven't got any flit guns,' I said, rather dimly.

'Then we'll have to buy some, won't we?' she said briskly.

And that's what we did. I drove the Land-Rover into Hillingdon and stopped at the first ironmonger's I saw.

'Do you stock flit guns?'

'Yes, I think I've still got some. There's not much call for them these days...'

'How many have you got?'

The ironmonger looked as if I'd gone mad, then, to humour me, disappeared into the back to rummage among the stock he never thought he'd sell. He came back. 'About half a dozen.'

'I'll take the lot.'

He knocked them down to me for a nominal shilling a time, probably to get rid of me, and I returned with the dusty, primitive fly-sprays to the Hostel.

We got the sugar solution ready, and sprayed the frames in turn. It was a long job. And a very messy one. Some of the solution got through the gauze. Most of it finished on the Hostel floor. The bees themselves got soaked and looked very bedraggled. But I hoped they enjoyed their unusual meal.

14

Fly Away Peter, Fly Away Paul

'The Athenaeum Club' was the most unlikely name the Hostel ever acquired, but it was accurate at certain times. Despite the frequent bustle when consignments of animals arrived or departed, the occasional trumpetings of elephants or snarls of tigers when they were in residence, and, most of all, the terrible racket of a thousand monkeys being fed, the atmosphere for a great deal of the time was tranquil, even serene. Birds and other creatures resting in their boxes, quite often asleep, gave rise to the name, because the Hostel then resembled nothing so much as a London club after luncheon. We didn't actually put newspapers over the faces of the sleeping inmates, nor did they snore over glasses of port; that, none the less, was the atmosphere.

One day the tranquillity was shattered. From my office I suddenly heard a terrified scream coming from down the corridor, and the direction of the end stable. I recognized one of the girl's voices. It was Anne McManus, who had been with us some time, but who always kept herself to herself.

'Help ... Mr Whittaker ... somebody ... come quickly ...' followed by quite anguished gasps and screams.

I dropped everything and ran from the office, covering the length of the corridor in a few seconds. In the far stable was a grotesque and frightening sight, like something out of Hitchcock's film *The Birds*. There was Anne only four-foot-ten hanging on for dear life to the huge shape of a Marabou stork, all five foot of it, with its great scavenging beak and powerful long, spindly legs, which could have dealt her a terrible blow. We had about thirty of these birds, carrion creatures from Africa, in the stable. They had travelled in containers which resembled great crates of hessian: they had hardboard floors and a frame, and were stretched round with sacking so that the birds would not damage themselves in transit. One of them had found its way out through a hessian side that was damaged.

Anne had been working in the stable when suddenly she heard an ominous movement and flapping and was confronted by this great primitive-looking creature. She had immediately grabbed the end of its long beak, and held on to its body, as well as trying to make sure she kept out of the way of its legs – not only for her own safety, but also, brave girl, to make sure that the bird did not damage itself while loose (something which could all too easily happen, because of the length of the stork's legs).

As I arrived, the stork was trying to prise the enormous point of its beak out of Anne's hand, swaying and hissing, and taking dangerous steps with its great claws. I arrived at the same time as two more of the girls, who had heard the screams; and not a moment too soon. We threw open the door of the stable just in time to see Anne's strength give out; she released a gaping beak as she collapsed to the floor. But her luck was in. The opening of the door threw light into the dimness of the stable, and the stork was distracted. He saw a chance of further freedom, and before we knew what was happening he was past us, through the door, and along the corridor.

'You get after him,' I shouted, 'I'll see to Anne.'

But Anne was up on her feet. 'I'm all right, really,' she said breathlessly, and we both turned and chased down the corridor after the other girls and the Marabou stork, who had turned into the kitchen.

With the danger over, it now seemed more like a Keystone comedy than the Hammer horror scene that could have taken place. As we ran into the kitchen, we were just in time to see the stork scrambling, half-flying, over the stainless steel sinks towards the open windows and the sunshine beyond. I lunged forward and made a grab at its legs. Too late. The stork had gone; not pausing to look round on the grass outside, it was airborne in a few feet. It soared up and flew powerfully off, heading in the direction of Stanwell Moor.

'Well, what do we do now?' I said, gazing through the window at the disappearing 'guest' and addressing myself more than anyone else. No one had any bright ideas.

By this time the stork was over a patch of waste ground that was cultivated as a market garden. About an acre of it was given over to growing maize. The tall, feathery fronds were at their height, since it was high summer, and perhaps the sight of them persuaded the stork that he was back in Africa. Whatever the reason, he began to circle, losing height, and then landed right in the middle of the maize plantation.

'Come on,' I said, 'now we can get him.' We all careered out of the kitchen, almost knocking over Graham Joss, one of the airline veterinary consultants who had arrived late on the scene to see what all the panic was about. Mr Joss, apart from being a vet in his own right, was B.O.A.C.'s veterinary consultant, and also on the Livestock Panel of I.A.T.A. He wasn't one of our greatest fans and didn't much approve of the Hostel, yet without a word he joined us now. Outside the Hostel, as we piled aboard the Land-Rover, we were joined by two airport police on motor-cycles, who had arrived quite by chance.

So this strange posse jolted away from the Hostel, and set off in a cloud of dust towards the maize patch where – somewhere – the Marabou stork was undoubtedly enjoying its unexpected freedom. 'We'll soon have him back,' I said confidently, as I parked the Land-Rover on the edge of the market garden area, 'that is, unless he takes off again.'

How wrong I was. We all fanned out to cover the maximum area, but after two hours, and a series of false alarms, the stork was still uncaptured. Looking for pygmies in tall elephant grass would have been simple by comparison. From time to time there would be a shout of 'There he is', and we would all concentrate, only to find that what had been sighted was no more than a particularly high frond of waving corn. Once one of the policeman did see the stork, but by the time we'd reached the place of the sighting the bird was hidden again. The only light relief was a terrible unconscious pun made by Mr Joss, in the depths of the maize: 'It's like Hampton Court Maze,' he called over to me.

'I think we're going to have to give up,' I said, 'and hope he comes out into more open ground.' By now it was mid-afternoon. Everyone was exhausted. The police had returned to less energetic ways of combating crime. But, no sooner had I decided to abandon the search than I heard a triumphant cry from about thirty yards away. 'I've got him. Lend a hand...'

It was Graham Joss. We all dashed in the direction of the shout, and, turning down one of the avenues which bisected the plantation, were in time to see the vet tying the beak of a quite unabashed and apparently docile stork with a piece of crêpe bandage he obviously carried with him for emergencies such as this. Back at the hostel we got the stork back in its crate and made sure the hessian was repaired and secure. We recovered with strong draughts of tea, and, at last, the silence of the Athenaeum returned.

The adventure with the Marabou stork, which could have ended so differently and with serious consequences for Anne, took place when the quarantine regulations were not as tight as they became later, and are now. When they were tightened up, there were some strange incidents as a result: as when the Pan-Am Clipper arrived with the Great Bertino, Illusionist and Magician Supreme, straight from Broadway, for a Limited Season Only in Britain.

Unfortunately, his season was limited in a sense he hadn't thought of. The Great Bertino's act depended very much on clever concealment about his person of a great variety of livestock, including rabbits for the classic out-of-the-hat routine, and doves to be 'discovered' in quantity under his cloak and released in a manner that recalled the famous old act by Kardomah who was billed 'He Fills the Stage with Flags'. Bertino, by contrast, filled the stage with doves.

The Great Bertino brought his own rabbits and doves with him on the Clipper, and, because no one had warned him about U.K. quarantine regulations, was as astonished as one of his own audiences when the Customs did their own vanishing trick before his very eyes, impounded the rabbits and doves, and had them sent down to us. I felt very sorry for the little magician, who, despite his name, was Brooklyn through and through.

Remembering my own time with an animal act in variety I felt very sympathetic towards him. I explained as gently as I could: the rabbits had to go into quarantine for six months, or go straight back to the States, or be put down. That was the law. The doves, meanwhile, had a 35-day quarantine 'sentence'.

'But I must have them for my act,' he said hopelessly, while his two handsome little white rabbits twitched their noses anxiously, and the doves cooed and fluttered about their cages.

In the end I convinced him that there really was no way round the quarantine regulations, but I suggested a reliable big firm of pet dealers in East London where I was sure he would be able to get two more white rabbits and as many doves as he wanted. No doubt there would be a training problem, but it would be better than no act at all.

So off he went, a little less dejected than when he had arrived at the Hostel. We, meanwhile, kept his rabbits and doves, applying to the Ministry for an extension for them after forty-eight hours, the statutory limit on the period we were supposed to have them. The rabbits became favourites in the Hostel and someone gave them names: Robby and Nobby.

Just over a month later the Great Bertino returned to claim his doves, their quarantine period having expired. At the same time he asked if he could have a look at his rabbits. When he saw Robby and Nobby he got a shock: from being little balls of fur no longer than eight inches, they were well on the way to becoming very mature white rabbits, of a size suitable for Alice in Wonderland, but no longer of any use for a magician, however supreme.

'Jeez,' exclaimed the Great Bertino, 'They're monsters! They don't make the size of top hat they'd fit into. What are we going to do?'

We had a long discussion, during which Robby and Nobby munched unconcernedly through their cabbage. In the end, the Great Bertino proved as good as his name. He promised to pay the quarantine boarding fees for them until their six months were up, so long as we could find them a suitable home. And this we did. Reg Childs, a Press photographer whom I knew, said he would take them for his eleven-year-old son – and, being a photographer, he eventually sent us some striking photographs of Robby and Nobby (later renamed) to show that they lived happily ever after. The Great Bertino, meanwhile, flew back to the States with his doves who, presumably, continued their stage career where they left off, on Broadway.

Magicians' doves, and doves used in other variety acts, did in fact become quite frequent visitors to the Hostel. But not all were pure white, like the Great Bertino's: we had shocking pink doves, lime green doves, powder blue doves, and forever amber doves – all dyed, of course. It was a practice deplored by the R.S.P.C.A., but there was not much we could do about it. It was difficult to prove that a particular dye was harmful to the bird, and cruelty itself was even more difficult to establish. Once again, the Customs were the first line of defence in intercepting.

They invariably came in carried in personal baggage, and the Customs men – particularly Old Crusty – seemed to have radar eyes when it came to doves and variety artistes' luggage.

Once intercepted, we kept them, with Ministry permission, in quarantine for the statutory period, feeling rather sorry that someone had sought to improve on nature. Apart from that, we kept an eye on the doves to see if they developed any symptoms of illness because of the dyeing, and, naturally, saw that the birds did not take a bath in case the dye came off and there were consequent ill-effects.

Our many-coloured pastel doves, nevertheless, were not the prize exhibits in our experience of dyed birds: this honour was awarded always on a Saturday during the Rugby season when France was playing England at Twickenham, or occasionally when France was playing Wales at Cardiff Arms Park. Planeloads of supporters came over from Orly. With them, invariably, were a few live cockerels, dyed red and blue on their native white to make the genuine Tricolour of the French national emblem.

However, concealed in holdalls, or under bulging raincoats and swirling rugby supporter scarves, they hardly stood a chance at the Customs, and none at all if Old Crusty was on duty. Which he mostly made a point of being: I'm told he used to ring the rugby dates on the calendar and even swap shifts to make sure he was at the barricades when the French flew in. It was like the Battle of Mons all over again, only better, because this time he was fighting against the French instead of with them!

But I'm not sure he didn't get an even bigger kick at the thought of giving us some unnecessary work. He would wait until the last dispossessed French fan had disappeared towards Twickenham or Paddington, then count his red, white and blue haul, and give us a gleeful ring. 'Got another lot of Froggy cock-a-doodle-doos for you. Make sure you look after them.'

We would curse the French, and Old Crusty, in that order and prepare to receive some sorry-looking national emblems. We shouldn't have cursed him, I suppose. It wasn't the colour that mattered, red, white, blue or sky-blue pink; it was that poultry, fowls, etc., were not allowed into the U.K. except under special licence.

We held the French cockerels until after the game, when the owners could come and collect them. There was never so much as a Gallic shrug of remorse or regret at the way they'd treated the birds, and I was always particularly glad when they'd lost. I also idly wondered what the French would have done in similar circumstances – that is if a load of English supporters on their way to the Parc des Princes for the return match had tried to smuggle in some red, white and blue lions!

Neither the French rugby supporters' cockerels, however, nor the artificially coloured magicians' doves, gave us our biggest headache in our dealings with dyed birds. We had to deal with an enormous traffic in dyed finches. Thousands upon thousands came through for the pet trade both in this country and in America and elsewhere; hundreds upon hundreds never lived to see a shop window, let alone a cage for somebody's living room.

It was all excused with the age-old commercial bromide: 'Oh, but there's a market for it.' One of the main sources of these birds was Taiwan. As many as 500 finches at a time were put in cages, and the cages were then dipped in vats of dye. Those birds that survived, inhaling the chemical, or swallowing it, or having their beaks choked with it, were then dried off and exported in their false colours. No wonder the International Society for the Protection of Animals could comment: 'The fatalities in finches are so high that it makes other mortality statistics look puny.' Calcutta, already mentioned as a plague spot for animal dealings, was another centre. The dark, evil-smelling so-called New Market, which had the reputation of being an 'animal Belsen', was the place the finches came from; they were stacked in cages, and sprayed with stirrup pumps, or simply had buckets of dye thrown over them.

At our end, we became accustomed to the sad sight of

these little painted birds, and the inevitable task whenever a consignment came in of removing those that had not arrived alive at Heathrow. Representations were continually being made, but they never had much effect. And the irony that crowned the entire business was that whoever was idiot enough to buy a dyed finch, attracted by its bright scarlet, green or blue, was doomed to find that in the process of moulting, within a short time, the little bird would revert at last to its natural state, a plain, ordinary, sooty brown. In which plumage, were it not for the whims of supposedly civilized society, it would still be fluttering in the trees of India and South-east Asia.

Meanwhile there was a problem with finches nearer home. We became worried because we discovered that bullfinches, goldfinches and greenfinches, all protected British wild birds, were being trapped and sold through the pet trade. There was a mystery element to all this (which started only in very recent years): the British finches were invariably found in the possession of passengers returning to Malta. What would happen would be that a Maltese passenger would report at Terminal Two, and in their luggage would be a small, usually crudely made cage, or even an ordinary shoebox with air-holes in it. In the security check it would be discovered what the contents were, and they would be confiscated, always amid protests that the passenger possessed a perfectly legal order to import the birds into Malta.

We never solved the mystery of why the Maltese in particular wanted to take these British birds back with them, or where they got them from, because by the time the security people had alerted us the passengers would have accepted that they could do nothing about the confiscation and would be on board their aircraft on their way home. It was a worrying business, the more so because there were signs that a regular trade in the birds was developing. Not merely single finches were recovered: we had cases of twenty or thirty birds at once. But no one to question.

When we got the birds down to the Hostel they were

let out into our release cages and kept as quiet as possible because they had already suffered by being taken from their wild state into captivity under conditions at which one can only hazard a guess. I would then contact the R.S.P.C.A. inspector at Windsor, who would come down, confirm that they were protected birds, and take them away for release back into their natural environments.

To try and solve the mystery we got in touch with the R.S.P.C.A. branch in Malta, but they couldn't throw any light on the business. And the airlines themselves were even more positively unhelpful when I tried to suggest a way of at least arresting the traffic. My idea was to have notices prominently displayed at Luqa Airport warning that it was illegal to take protected birds out of England. No good. Equally unacceptable was my suggestion that incoming flights from Malta to Heathrow should be warned. 'No,' said the airlines, 'not our policy.'

It was all very frustrating.

15

Malta Airlift

The unsolved mystery of the British finches was not the Hostel's only dealing with Malta. In January 1972 I was flown out there by Trident to assist in an emergency operation to rescue pets affected by the evacuation of 1,500 Service families. The Maltese Prime Minister, Dom Mintoff, had decreed 'troops out', and this had brought an unforeseen problem in its wake. Easy enough, perhaps, to get the troops home. But many of the soldiers, sailors and airmen had permanent quarters amounting to homes in Malta. And with the homes, as in Britain, went dogs, cats, and assorted hamsters and budgies.

To take their pets with them, however, cost a lot of money in air fares, and if they didn't take them humane destruction was the only alternative, barring the chance of finding some kindly disposed Maltese family. The Ministry of Defence said it could not foot the bill for pets to be flown to the U.K. and most of the Services pet owners simply couldn't afford the fares. Consequently there was a great deal of distress, and Mr Mintoff came in for some bitter criticism which had nothing to do with politics.

All this had a practical effect possible, perhaps, in no other country in the world. Back in Britain the R.S.P.C.A. were alerted to the situation. They went into action and launched an appeal through the Press for funds to save as many of the animals as possible. The Executive Director, Major Seager, appeared on television. There was an instant and amazing response. At the request of the Society, the Ministry of Agriculture and Fisheries approved temporary quarantine kennels at Godstone. The *Daily Mirror* weighed in by providing a B.E.A. aircraft to transport the animals. B.E.A. themselves provided crates and flew them out to Malta.

B.E.A. also made an approach to the R.S.P.C.A. asking for me to be flown out to Malta to supervise the boxing and crating of the pets, and look after them on the flight back. R.S.P.C.A. Headquarters agreed readily, and the message was passed down the line to the Hostel. Also details of the rather complicated provisions of my journey. B.E.A. had explained to the R.S.P.C.A.: 'Because of I.A.T.A. regulations we can't give Mr Whittaker a free ticket out to Malta. But we can give a rebate and fly him out as *our* consultant on a scheduled Trident. The flight back is slightly more difficult, because we'll be using a Vanguard freighter, which is a merchant aircraft and is not allowed passengers, even travelling as animal attendants. So Mr Whittaker will have to become a member of the crew – and to do that, if he agrees, we'll arrange for him to take the Board of Trade Survival Course and get his necessary certificate.'

I thought it a very clever way that B.E.A. had found through the red tape, and, thrilled at being asked to go and look after the Malta pets, I was also greatly pleased at the unexpected idea of becoming, after all these years of being in contact with them, an actual member of an aircraft's crew. So I reported to the training centre at Ruislip, and did a rapid course on simulated flight-decks, finding out what to do in an emergency: where the axes were, where the exits were, what the emergency drills were, how the oxygen supply worked, and where the dinghy was stowed in case we had to ditch. Everything, in fact, except how to try and save the animal cargo should the need arise.

The R.S.P.C.A. had launched its appeal on Friday, 7 January, and by the following Tuesday, 11 January, I was airborne. Shortly afterwards, I was checking into the Floriana Hotel, and later in the afternoon reporting to the local R.S.P.C.A. It was arranged that I should be down at their quarantine kennels at 5 a.m. the following morning to begin my work.

In between, the time was my own. I decided I would have a look round Valetta, and in particular the Grand Harbour. I'd not been there since my time in the Royal Navy, and, despite many a 'run ashore' there, I'd never much liked the place, a view shared with not a few of my old mess-mates. I know Malta took a lot of punishment during the war from German air raids, and for this was awarded the George Cross as an island – hence Malta G.C. – but the tradesmen ashore were masters at ripping you off long before the phrase was ever invented. Somehow they scented that the Fleet was coming in, and up would go prices all round. The mess caterers would come back on board after a hard morning earning their pay bargaining. 'Shave off,'* they would say, 'guess what those [expletive deleted] Malts are asking for [expletive deleted] spuds?'

I wondered if the place had improved with its independence and its big tourism drive. When I got to a point where I could see the harbour, I got a shock. As I remembered it from thirty and more years previously, from the entrance breakwaters to Customs House jetty and the great fort of St Angelo, built by the Knights of Malta, which dominated the harbour, there were Royal Navy ships as far as the eye could see: battle-cruisers and battleships from *Repulse* to *Revenge*, aircraft-carriers from *Furious* to *Ark Royal*, countless cruisers, and, in Sliema Creek, destroyers and smaller ships by the score.

But, as I looked over the expanse of blue in the later afternoon sun in January 1972, there wasn't a White Ensign in sight. The biggest ship in a near-empty Grand Harbour, and a sign of the times, was a Soviet cruise-liner, hammer and sickle prominent on its funnel.

I turned quite sadly away and went back to the Floriana for a meal. That and a drink revived me, and, I thought, there's the rest of the evening. I planned another latter-day 'run ashore'. The place we always used to

*Common naval expression of exasperation.

make for was a street known as The Gut in the middle of Valetta. I remembered it of old as narrow and full of noise, sailors, girls, drunks, naval shore patrols being kept busy, bar after bar with open fronts, clip joints, honky tonks, and houses of very ill-fame. I now decided to see what it was like in 1972.

I set off into the maze of bustling, brightly lit medieval streets, and came to what we used to call The Gut. I looked along it, and – something that could never have been done when I was there last – could see from end to end. It was deserted, and silent. Another illusion gone. But I decided I might as well have a walk along it for old time's sake, and when I did I was surprised to find that the bars still existed. Not only that, they still had their old names, and were open. I thought, picking among half-remembered familiar places, I would try The Warspite Bar for size.

It hadn't changed, not in appearance anyhow. But, like The Gut itself, it was deserted, not a customer in sight. Behind the bar, knitting, sat a large Maltese lady in the usual large black dress. I nearly turned round straight away, but then I thought I might as well have a beer. When it had been poured for me, in silence, I took it across to the wall which was still covered with photographs of ships' companies, a lot of them from before the war, and before the time I'd joined the Navy.

They'd faded and gone brown over the intervening years, and the flies had done their best to try and obliterate them. But they were still there. H.M.S. *Warspite*'s officers and men, 1936, rows of cheerful grinning faces; similar but sadder, a long photograph of the ship's company of the biggest warship in the world, H.M.S. *Hood*. It was taken in 1938, three years before she'd been sunk with only two survivors out of more than a thousand. There was even the cruiser H.M.S. *Devonshire* in which I served, but it must have been taken before I joined. I couldn't recognize anyone. I finished my beer quickly. I wanted to leave. The Warspite Bar was becoming a ghostly place.

So I went back along The Gut heading for the hotel,

and came across the only activity of my entire evening. From an upstairs window ahead I heard the tinkle of a piano. As I passed I saw it was coming from a dimly pink-lit room. On the balcony were two girls, both of them dark and pretty, with black dresses of a more fashionable cut than the one in The Warspite Bar.

'Wanta nice time with us?' came the inevitable invitation.

'No thanks, love.'

I passed on. At least this hadn't changed.

Then, two paces further on, I heard something that gave me a bigger surprise and more pleasure than anything else in my entire Malta visit. My ears were assailed by a great yell from one of the girls.

'Shave off!' she shouted.

It was incredible. She'd seen my beard. Young as she was she knew the right phrase. The Navy was not completely forgotten in Valetta after all.

It was as well we started early: it was a full day's work supervising the loading and correct labelling of all the pets, a total of 184 of them, and getting them down to the airport in transport provided by the Army. And then, just as we were ready to start loading up the Vanguard, Malta gave a final farewell kick to the servicemen it was throwing out. A Mediterranean winter downpour soaked the tie-on destination labels on the crates and boxes, and many of them were totally obscured. It was something we couldn't do anything about at the time. The quarantine manager who had arranged the labelling was frantic, but I had to tell him, 'Never mind. It's not the end of the world. We'll sort it all out at Heathrow.' Quite how we would sort it out I had no idea, but sorted out it would assuredly have to be, and in the meantime I wanted some sleep.

Early next morning I reported to the Vanguard in my new capacity of crew member. The captain greeted me with due gravity. I met the engineer and second pilot and took my seat, casting my freshly acquired professional eye around and noting that everything, down to the last emergency axe, seemed to be where I expected it to be from my brief training at Ruislip. It was a totally different feeling sitting there waiting for engine start and watching the captain do his pre-flight checks, totally unlike being a passenger. 'Check seat-belts,' said the captain as, by now, the big turbo-props were ticking over. What the captain said next, however, prevented me becoming too airborne with myself. Turning back in his seat, he said, 'Neville, the important thing is to forget all you were told on your survival course. Don't do anything. We'll tell you what to do if anything goes wrong. Whatever you do, don't go pressing any buttons or doing anything you think you might have to do. Just leave it to us.'

I was a bit deflated, but forgot soon enough when we lined up on the main runway at Luqa, and I saw for the first time what take-off is really like from the front seat. Why hadn't I done this sort of thing before? It beat the roller coaster at Blackpool by a million miles. And, once airborne, everything was so different. I looked out and down, and there below was Malta dropping astern, and by the minute more and more resembling a piece of bath-brick set in a sea of grey.

For some reason I didn't put my earphones on immediately, but I could see that the captain had suddenly become seriously engaged in conversation with the engineer. He turned abruptly and signalled me to put my earphones on. They were shaking their heads. My heart gave a thump. Something had gone wrong. This was the emergency, and I had to leave it all to them. I heard a crackling in the earphones and caught the tail end of their grave conversation.

'You're joking,' the captain was saying, 'We'll murder them in the line-out...'

Then I remembered there was a Rugby International at Twickenham in two days' time.

'Neville,' said the captain, looking round again to see I was plugged in, 'you can go down aft now if you like to see how everything is.'

Breathing freely once more, I made my way through the crew door into the big compartment. There stretched box after box of dogs and cats; fortunately the rain had not affected the identity labels on all their crates, so I was able to see that they were all right, and in many cases know by name who was asleep, who wagged his tail at the sight of me, and which cat wanted to claw its way out to greet me. I inspected every one of my charges, opening the boxes and giving them all a pat or a stroke. They all seemed very relaxed, and none more so than one of the budgies whom I discovered to be sitting tight in her nesting box on three eggs.

Back on the flight-deck the routine went on. Darkness fell, and the cockpit lighting came on. Then, in no time at all it seemed, we were banking through a hole in the cloud, and below us were jumbled necklaces of light getting closer. We were on the east-west approach to Heathrow. Once again, being up front, I was fascinated. The approach lights, lines and bars grew bigger and bigger. The runway looked more and more like a giant illuminated plank being steadily canted up to meet us, and growing in size all the time. Then we were down, with a landing that would not have disturbed one sleeping cat.

We taxied in. The freight doors were opened. The January air hit us. I was amazed to see an immense crowd of press and cameramen waiting for us, and the glare of television lights. We were, so I read the following day, the 'Mercy Mission From Malta'. But standing there on the steps of the Vanguard I was astonished at the reception.

The flight was over, but my work was not. The unloading had to be supervised, in particular the budgie with her eggs, then transit to the Hostel. By the end of the evening we were full of crates, all of them marked at least 'Scottie', 'Dachshund', 'Yellow Labrador', or 'Tabby', 'Black with White Tuft', 'Tortoiseshell'. The following day we were contacted by the owners, and the tangle, by no means as serious as we had anticipated in Malta, with the smudged labels was sorted out.

Less than a week before, Malta could hardly have been further from my thoughts. Now, despite the feelings I used to have about the place, I was proud to have been there, and even more proud that I had taken part in a unique operation. Of course, this was not reported in the Press. I leave it to the *R.S.P.C.A. News* to give a more factual and sober appraisal of the Malta Animal Airlift: 'On Thursday, January 13, Mr Whittaker accompanied a consignment of 184 dogs, cats and birds, which arrived safely after an uneventful journey. He said, "It was a smooth flight, which most of the animals spent sleeping."'

16

Thirty Years On

As we went on into the seventies, the Hostel was still in full swing. But the pattern was changing. The monkey trade was at last petering out. The big jets were playing an ever more important part in making life better for the animals who travelled by air. The public were becoming more and more aware of the need to protect and conserve wild life. This in its turn was having its effect in diminishing the traffic in animals. In addition, and partly owing to our own efforts, the authorities had been made so alive to the plight of airborne livestock that the decade saw an important series of legal measures. These, in the end, reduced the number of animals being transported so much that the Hostel was no longer a necessity. By an ironic stroke we had become our own executioners – though with no regrets.

Already, in 1969, under strong pressure from the R.S.P.C.A. and other bodies, I.A.T.A, the official organization regulating all aspects of airline operation, had brought out its own manual covering the transport of animals by air. It extended the advice given in the earlier B.S.I. handbook, and, unlike that document, had application outside Great Britain. It was not binding on members, but it was a big step in the right direction. It took several years more before I.A.T.A. finally made the advice into mandatory regulations that all its members had to obey. But shortly before that happened some real teeth were provided as far as Great Britain and, in particular, the R.S.P.C.A. were concerned, in the shape of the Transit of Animals (General) Order 1973. This Act of Parliament at last gave us a real weapon with which to fight the particular kind of cruelty we encountered. If exporters of animals chose to ignore the advice that was freely available to them, and the airlines condoned their malpractice by carrying the cargo, the airlines themselves were liable to prosecution. The Act was quite simple and straightforward, and applied to animals carried by any means whatsoever. It laid down that a container had to be big enough for a given species, not overcrowded, and with proper provision for ventilation, food and water. It also had to be properly labelled. It was what we'd been fighting for over more than twenty years.

Our side of it was covered by the section dealing with 'Animals in Receptacles'. The onus for ensuring the regulations were observed fell upon 'The person in charge at the time', which, in our case, meant the airlines. It was no use henceforward their saying: 'We didn't know the animals were being transported like this.' No matter that it was a freight clerk had let them aboard an airliner, the airline could be fined, and the implication was that the animals should never have been allowed on board their aircraft in the first place.

However, the method by which the prosecutions had to be brought led to a curious sequence of events whenever we were involved. This arose from the fact that local authorities were held to be responsible for administration of the Act. London Airport, curiously enough, came under the jurisdiction of the Port of London Authority. In turn, this meant that the Corporation of the City of London was the local authority responsible for bringing any prosecution. In practice, this meant that whenever we came across a case that was, in our R.S.P.C.A. view, deserving of prosecution, I would have to phone the City. An inspector would be sent down to investigate, and one of their veterinary surgeons. Evidence would be taken from the staff at the Hostel and cargo handlers at the airport, and the City of London's legal department would then decide whether to proceed and have a summons served on the airline concerned. If the case proceeded, I would then appear as a prosecution witness, and at this point the I.A.T.A. manual became invaluable, because it provided the guidelines laid down for the ideal carriage of animals by air.

The first case ever brought under the Act gave great satisfaction at the Hostel. At last we felt we were *doing* something other than make either deprecatory or advisory noises. By a strange coincidence it was also an unbelievably fitting case for the R.S.P.C.A. to be involved in.

According to the R.S.P.C.A.'s records, the first successful case ever brought before a magistrate concerning cruelty to animals was in 1823. A man actually brought his donkey into court to show the injuries and demonstrate the palpable cruelty that had been inflicted. A conviction resulted.

Almost exactly 150 years later I appeared in the witness box at Uxbridge Magistrates Court in the first case we helped to bring under the new Act, and, once again, it concerned a donkey. This little animal had been flown in from Ireland for onward transit abroad in a slatted crate (not the kind of solid box that was recommended). It was so small that the donkey couldn't even put his neck forward properly. In addition, the crate was tacky with fresh creosote, which did nothing for the poor animal's coat, which happened to be white.

This was the first of many, many times I appeared in that same court over the next few years, in a succession of cases that were won under the new Act. The donkey was the first beneficiary of the legislation, but a host of animals and birds followed, right the way through the range of beasts, including bears, lions, and tigers.

Something had been achieved at last, and gradually the Act itself had a long-term effect to the benefit of the animals. In addition to this Act, quarantine regulations for the U.K. were tightened and extended, and in 1976 another piece of legislation reached the statute book which was to have a big effect on our activities. This was the Dangerous Wild Animals Act of 1976. These measures did much to cut down the kind of creature allowed freely into the U.K., and hence that we would handle.

As the seventies progressed, the number of animals coming through steadily declined, so that by 1980 it was a mere trickle, compared with the flood we had been so used to. Our work was nearly over. This was sad in one way, but immensely satisfactory in another. We had the knowledge that much unnecessary suffering had been prevented by our earlier activities. We also had a total of seventeen million living creatures to show for our work, three-quarters of a million of them monkeys – a figure that would have been several million higher had I ever bothered the staff to waste time and return statistics of all the tropical fish we handled.

As some indication of how long we had been in business I was able to glance at our latest bed-and-breakfast charges at the Hostel: Elephant (large) £30, Elephant (small) £20, Baboon £10, Vulture £3, Snake (requiring handling) £3.50, Snake (not requiring handling) 75p. A far cry from the early days when the fees were calculated in pence rather than pounds, and a large elephant would have existed for several months on the fees we had to charge by 1980. But by then the R.S.P.C.A. was losing no less than £40,000 a year on the Hostel, and I had been asked to fix the scale of charges so that at least we got something back.

In 1981 the Hostel closed its doors for ever. The animal cargoes coming through Heathrow by then were no longer sufficient to warrant the R.S.P.C.A.'s expense in keeping it open. I was not present to witness the last rites. Early in 1980 I had retired to my cottage in Wiltshire, and said goodbye to an extraordinary life, and an extraordinary routine – if that's not too stiff a word – of laughter, pathos, hard work, and, in the early days, all too frequent horror. I also said goodbye to the girls that remained, with the thought that the M.B.E. I had been honoured with in 1978 belonged just as much to them and their predecessors, proud as I was of it. Another honour of which I was equally proud was the Queen Victoria Silver Medal awarded me by the R.S.P.C.A. It is the highest award of the Society and no words could express how I felt when I received it.

Sometimes, looking back, it all seems a dream, and the Hostel another location for Alice in Wonderland. Was I really called out in the small hours of one winter morning to meet an aircraft from Rome which had reported two tigers broken out in the hold? The cargo doors had been opened, and then shut very smartly when the contents were seen to be striped, snarling, and on the loose. At Heathrow (it was before the days of dart guns) I managed to inject them with tranquillizer in the paws.

Did an alligator really arrive with its snout bound round with coils of stout manila rope? With true R.S.P.C.A. feeling we unwound the rope and gave the big reptile full freedom to flex its jaws again – out of range. Then came the difficulties and dangers of re-crating it. This was achieved by packing other boxes around and behind him so that gradually he was shifted forward and coaxed (not quite the word for an alligator, but it will have to do) back into his travelling container. The tail-gate was then slammed firmly shut.

Did I really intervene to save the life of a turtle? An anonymous caller gave us a tip-off, and I went down to the unloading bays where an aircraft was drawn up, doors open, and round it enough press and photographers to suggest at least royalty arriving, or possibly the Rolling Stones. But neither H.M. the Queen nor Mick Jagger was anywhere in sight. From the 707 stepped some men with a large turtle. The whole thing was a publicity stunt for a big banquet. But the ultimate fate of the turtle was not my first concern as I saw it being landed: its front flippers and legs were tied very tightly with rough cord, and round its neck was a sort of lasso that was biting into its flesh. The intention, apparently, was to put this poor creature on an outsize silver salver to be photographed for the benefit of the catering firm before being despatched to be made into soup.

I quickly went into action with a protest to the P.R. man in charge, and made it clear that if the animal wasn't taken down to our Hostel immediately to be released I would do all I could to ensure prosecution for cruelty. At this an airline official who was in on the conversation made some suitably soothing noises, and the P.R. man said that since I put it like that he had no option but to call the whole thing off. An announcement was made to the Press, who by now were getting impatient. They shrugged their shoulders and went off to other assignments. I drove off triumphantly in the R.S.P.C.A. ambulance with one turtle, trying to fathom as I did so the mentality of whoever had dreamt up such a weird and callous stunt.

Once into the Hostel we cut the cords, and fed the turtle, who was obviously starving – unlike his predecessors of years ago, when it was general practice, apparently, to pack turtles as ballast in the holds of ships, and, to improve their ultimate flavour, to feed them champagne, no expense spared. Also unlike his predecessors we managed to ensure that he had a happier future than being turned into soup.

It is hardly surprising that I sit in my armchair these days and wonder whether it all really happened. When I doze off I have strange dreams: dreams which feature not only unimaginable events, but events on an incredible scale – like a fog-shrouded Heathrow with the looming lights of the Land-Rovers of farmer friends from Wiltshire, who had somehow managed to drive up to help me out. We had 84,000 day-old chicks on our hands, the biggest export consignment ever, and so delayed by the fog that it was finally useless attempting to send them abroad.

Day-old chicks can't be kept for more than forty-eight hours without full-time care, otherwise they are in danger. The Hostel was full to overflowing with them, stacked everywhere, and all at risk if we couldn't find new owners for them. The chicks were nearly all future broilers, and although we managed to place thousands through normal trade channels with the help of the exporters, there were still thousands left over.

So I put in a call to my local pub. The message was relayed to local farmers, who dropped everything to

come up to Heathrow through the fog in an extraordinary rescue operation which, years later, is still remembered – and not a chick was lost. The next day brought 5,000 wrongly routed lobsters to inspect, and not long afterwards a call from Air Canada. Would we look at 8,000 eels on their way to Belgium to see if they were fit to travel, because a previous consignment had arrived in poor condition? Many hours later the girls and I were able to report back that the 8,000 eels were indeed O.K. and on their way.

With these dreams came other strange parades: of animals who wanted to be stowaways – dogs, cats, rats, snakes who had somehow got into aircraft holds, once even a praying mantis – and endless passengers with an ambition to be small-scale smugglers: two German students attempting to take king snakes in their suitcases back to Düsseldorf, many a 'pregnant' woman with a cat concealed under her dress, scores of people hiding boxes containing hamsters, tortoises and budgies, and a Pakistani who wanted to take a stick insect home as a pet. Professional smugglers had other ways. It was nothing to open a box marked 'Water Fowl' and find rare pygmy geese. Or one labelled 'Crows', and discover birds of paradise. Labelling could never be taken for granted as one girl found when she opened a crate one day, anticipating from its markings a 'baby elly'. Out stepped a Shetland pony.

Did we really have a gorilla driven off from the Hostel by a chauffeur in a Silver Wraith Rolls-Royce? We did, several times; all the gorillas belonged to John Aspinall, the casino man and animal collector. Was there really a duck-billed platypus who could be tempted only with earthworms from the paddock and king prawns from the deep-freeze?

And did we really come across £30,000 worth of marijuana thrown on the Hostel tip? We did: it had arrived in crates containing Alsatians. The smuggling technique was discovered when larger boxes were found for the dogs to continue their journey in and the old crates went on the tip. When their metal lids were prised off so that the crates could be burnt, secret compartments were revealed containing the drugs.

Sick animals we also had by the score; some of them now seem to belong to the realm of fantasy. Did we really have a sick sea cow on our hands? Yes, we did, and it was at once the most unusual creature we ever saw at the Hostel, and the most pathetic. A low-loader and fork-lift truck arrived one day, and it looked at first sight as if another elephant had arrived. But the crate contained a steel frame, slings, and canvas. In the canvas was this enormous seal-like creature, a bit of water lapping round it. It was a manatee, or sea cow.

I thought at first that it was a dead sea cow. There was no sign of life whatsoever; its huge, shiny bulk lay motionless. I touched it, and there was no reaction. But at least its eyes were open, and I thought I just detected a flicker. By this time word had got round the Hostel, and all the girls had turned out to see our most extraordinary guest being unloaded. We had it taken to our aquatic section and the first thing we did was to change the murky water it had arrived in. Fortunately the manatee is a fresh-water creature; I gathered it had come from South America, where it lives in the estuaries of rivers such as the Amazon. The next problem was what to feed it on. Its natural food was river vegetation, which accounts at least for the 'cow' part of its name. Somehow, by sending out to pet shops, we managed to get hold of some aquatic weeds that we hoped would be a good substitute.

But the creature showed no interest at all. All day it lay there unblinking and unmoving, the weeds untouched. We were in despair, and very sad. In all my years at the Hostel I had never seen such a pathetic sight; I couldn't help thinking of it back in its own home estuary, happily being mistaken for a mermaid by passing sailors. Finally we decided to try it on lettuce.

Next morning when I came in, Maureen met me in a state of great excitement. 'I think some of the lettuce has gone,' she said.

I immediately went down to have a look. The sea cow was still motionless, but it certainly looked as if some of the lettuce had disappeared.

The following day the news was even better. Most of the lettuce had definitely vanished. Our sea cow must have fed during the night. And by the time, a few hours later, that it was due to be flown out to Germany, destined for a zoo, it had blinked an eye. Nothing more, but the relief all round the Hostel could almost be felt.

Was it all a fantasy? I sometimes wonder, but beside the memories of sick animals I have one of a sick human being which gave me nightmares. A puppy had been brought in from France illegally by some people who didn't know the quarantine laws. They could afford neither the quarantine fees nor its fare back to France. The only alternative was to have the dog, intended as a present for a little girl, humanely put down. And this they chose to have done. But the story somehow got into the Press. Two days later I had a letter with a scrawled address, simply 'Neville Whittaker, R.S.P.C.A., London.' It was a threat to murder me.

Looking back it seems that there were dangers enough in the Hostel without possible attempts on my life. Like the time we had a bottle-fed leopard cub in on its way to Edinburgh Zoo. The girls adored it, and looked after it continually. A week later we had a phone call to say the leopard cub had died – of rabies. All six girls who had been in contact with it had to have a very unpleasant course of anti-rabies injections, and all were made extremely anxious: the injections were no cure for this fatal illness, but simply lessened its painful effects. As the days passed watching for symptoms, we had a nerve-racking time, and only when the known period for incubation was over did we breathe freely again.

Then there was the time I was giving a 10-foot royal python a bath. It had also been delayed in transit, in this instance because of documentation. It was beginning to slough, and I decided I would give it a warm bath to help it get rid of its skin. Normally snakes are no trouble whatsoever to look after, but this one proved an exception; I was glad in retrospect it was not a poisonous variety. On one of my fingers I wear a rather heavy gold signet ring. This must somehow have attracted the python's attention, and he took against it and sank his fangs into my hand. Once again, it was the hospital for me – and this time for injections in a very unfashionable part of my anatomy. I had been scratched by lions, tigers, monkeys and bears, and pecked by parrots and one persistent ox-bird, it may be remembered, but this was the first time that I – or anyone else at the Hostel – had been bitten by a snake. Afterwards I knew that Cleopatra had not chosen an easy way to die.

Yet, snake bites, vultures in the night, and murder threats all included, I would willingly do it all over again. If we had these occasional dramas, we also had our compensations. We may not actually have rubbed shoulders with the royal, rich and famous, but we certainly had their animals and birds as our guests: from a canary belonging to the Queen to cheetahs given to the Duchess of Gloucester, and pigeons imported by the late Lord Mountbatten.

When we complained that some greyhounds belonging to an Arab sheikh were inhumanely crated and kept them, he paid for the re-crating and sent his own jet airliner to London to fetch them, also bringing some of his wives who wanted to go to Harrods. Lady Beaverbrook read about an animal that would have to be put down if quarantine fees could not be found. She paid. Vince Hill gave a little dog called Boots a new lease of life. It had been found in a boot-box abandoned on the airport – hence its name. Once again the Press made a story, and Vince Hill, reading the headlines, immediately phoned up to say he would pay the six-months' fee for the little puppy.

It all added to life at the Hostel, and, as I hope I've shown, that life never lacked for variety. Today the Hostel is silent, but its sounds remain in my mind, along with all the happy and sad times.

I can't say our cottage in the heart of Wiltshire is as silent, though. Outside, perhaps. Inside no. In addition to our two Boston terriers, and Ossie the tortoise, I have frequent friendly visitors on the doorstep – and sometimes over the doorstep – who come to be fed: Twink the chaffinch, Robbie the robin, Billy the sparrow, and Emmy the blackbird. It's not quite the Hostel all over again, but it keeps me in touch. And if, down the lane, I see my neighbouring farmer's pigs, there's something I know for sure about them. They really *can* fly. So can any animal, come to that.